I AM A MUSLIM

A MODERN STORYBOOK

(Based on the Qur'an, Hadith, and Stories of the Companions,
with Stories of Today's Muslim Children)

A Supplementary Social Studies Unit for Kindergarten

Written by Susan Douglass

Illustrated by Carol Joumaa

Goodwordkidz

Helping you build a family of faith

First published 1995 by
The International Institute of Islamic Thought (IIIT)
500 Grove St., 2nd Floor
Herndon, VA 20170-4735, USA
Tel: (1-703) 471 1133 / Fax: (1-703) 471 3922
E-mail: iiit@iiit.org / URL: http://www.iiit.org

First published by Goodword Books in 2003
Reprinted 2004
in arrangement with The International Institute of Islamic Thought
© The International Institute of Islamic Thought 1995

Goodword Books Pvt. Ltd.
1, Nizamuddin West Market
New Delhi 110 013
e-mail: info@goodwordbooks.com
Printed in India

www.goodwordbooks.com

IIIT is a cultural and intellectual foundation registered in the United States of America in 1981 with the objectives of providing a comprehensive Islamic outlook through elucidating the principles of Islam and relating them to relevant issues of contemporary thought; regaining the intellectual, cultural, and civilizational identity of the ummah through Islamization of the various disciplines of knowledge, to rectify the methodology of contemporary Islamic thought in order to enable it to resume its contribution to the progress of human civilization and give it meaning and direction in line with the values and objectives of Islam.

IIIT seeks to achieve its objectives by holding specialized academic seminars and conferences, supporting and publishing research works, supporting educational and cultural institutions and projects, supporting and guiding graduate and post-graduate studies.

The IIIT Islamic School Book Project supports the writing, publication, and distribution of books and other teaching material for schools as part of its effort to present the true picture of Islam in a factual objective way. These educational resources, developed under the general guidelines of the IIIT Islamization of Knowledge program, cover the following fields: Islamic Studies, Social Studies, Literature, Science and Mathematics. International collaboration and coordination with teachers, schools and organizations is assured through the International Forum for Education Resources for Islamic English-medium schools.

For more information contact:

The Director
IIIT Islamic School Book Project
International Institute of Islamic Thought (IIIT)
500 Grove St., 2nd Floor,
Herndon, VA 20170-4735, USA
Tel: (1-703) 471 1133 / Fax: (1-703) 471 3922
E-mail: iiit@iiit.org / URL: http://www.iiit.org

ABOUT THE AUTHOR

Susan Douglass is an American-born Muslim who accepted Islam in 1974. She received the Bachelor of Arts in History from the University of Rochester in 1972. She received the Master of Arts in Arab Studies from Georgetown University in 1992. She holds teaching certification in social studies from New York and Virginia.

She has taught in a variety of settings and subjects, beginning with volunteer work in Headstart in 1965. She taught and coordinated art classes in a summer youth program from 1970-72 in Rochester, NY. Since returning to the U.S. in 1984, from extended stays in Germany and Egypt, she resumed work in education. She has taught arts, crafts and story sessions in Muslim summer school programs for several years in Herndon, VA. As teacher and Head of the Social Studies Department at the Islamic Saudi Academy, Fairfax, VA, she taught both elementary and secondary social studies, built a supplementary resource library, and led in preparing a K-12 social studies curriculum utilizing both American and Arab resources for the Academy's accreditation. The current IIIT project was conceived and developed in the classroom. The author is involved in numerous other educational projects, including work as reviewer and consultant to major textbook publishers in the field of social studies. She has reviewed and offered revisions to the California History/Social Science Framework (1994) and the National History Standards Project (1994), in addition to various projects for the Council on Islamic Education in Fountain Valley, CA, including a book, *Strategies and Structures for Presenting World History, with Islam and Muslim History as a Case Study* (Council on Islamic Education, 1994.)

ADVISORY PANEL MEMBERS

Rahima Abdullah
Elementary Coordinator
Islamic Saudi Academy, Alexandria, VA

Dr. Kadija A. Ali
Educational Projects Coordinator
International Institute of Islamic Thought, Herndon, VA

Jinan N. Alkhateeb
Social Studies Teacher
Islamic Saudi Academy, Alexandria, VA

Mrs. Hamida Amanat
Director of Education
American Islamic Academy
Curriculum Consultant
Al-Ghazaly School, Pine brook, NJ

Shaker El Sayed
Coordinator
Islamic Teaching Center, Islamic Schools Department
Islamic Society of North America, Plainfield, IN

Dr. Tasneema Ghazi
IQRA International Educational Foundation, Chicago, IL

Dr. Zakiyyah Muhammad
Universal Institute of Islamic Education, Sacramento, CA

Many people's efforts have contributed to producing this series of supplementary units for Social Studies. First, I am grateful to the International Institute of Islamic Thought (IIIT) for placing their confidence in me to undertake a project of this size and for providing all the financial and logistical resources needed for its completion. I would like to thank Dr. Mahmud Rashdan, under whose guidance this project began in 1988. His wisdom helped to set it on a solid foundation. Without constant support and encouragement by Dr. Omar Kasule, project director 1991-present, and Dr. Khadija Ali Sharief, project coordinator (1993-present), this unit would never have met the light of day.

The project has been much enhanced by the members of the Advisory Panel. In addition to offering guidance on the project as a whole, they have spent much time and detailed effort on each individual manuscript. These brothers and sisters are all active education professionals with a broad range of experience and a long list of accomplishments.

May Allah reward my family and grant them patience for sacrificing some degree of comfort so that I, as wife and mother, might realize this goal. I owe special thanks to my husband, Usama Amer, for his constant help with the computer, with Arabic sources and many other matters of consultation. With regard to the writing and editing process, I thank the children, my own and those of my reviewers, who patiently listened to the stories, zeroing in on inconsistencies missed by their elders. I thank the parents who read with enthusiasm from a dry manuscript. They are Selma AbuGudiri, Tanweer Mirza and Mary Al-Khatib. I appreciate the enthusiam and patience of Khadijah Smith, who team-taught this unit with me during the 1993 Islamic Summer School at ADAMS Center in Herndon, VA. Gratitude is extended to Rabiah Abdullah, whose keen mind and sharp pencil have shaped and pruned text for the whole project, as well as lending her encouragement since its inception.

The illustrator, Carol Joumaa, worked skillfully and gracefully under pressure of the deadline. Appreciation goes to Nellie Al-Saigh, who helped with the Hajj diary in her usual prompt and energetic manner. Finally, thanks to the many people of Kendall-Hunt Publishing Co. who graciously met my many requests and turned tentative, complex and unfamiliar material into a finished product.

May Allah reward the efforts of all sincere workers and of the teachers and students for whom this unit was written.

Susan Douglass
Falls Church, Virginia
December 1994

TABLE OF CONTENTS

Part I:

Introduction for the Teacher

INTRODUCTION

This unit is Part 1 (kindergarten) of a 13-part series of units for use in Muslim school Social Studies programs. The underlying assumption is that most such schools will use mainstream curricula as a starting point. While it is certainly desirable and necessary to produce a complete Islamic Social Studies curriculum, it is a task which is best taken on step by step. In the meantime, it seems most productive to design supplements which are integrated into topics typically studied at a given grade level, while introducing content vital to the development of Muslim identity, values and world view. At the same time, it is hoped that the issues covered in these units are of such importance that they might in turn become integrated into a complete Islamic curriculum.

An important requirement in the design of this supplementary series is that each unit features skills and concepts typical for the scope and sequence of the social studies curriculum in its grade level. In this way, the teacher can introduce information about the Islamic heritage using material that is well integrated into the existing social studies program. This feature of the design also makes it possible to substitute this material for unsatisfactory or unnecessary material from standard textbooks, thus avoiding overburdening the students.

UNIT OVERVIEW

This unit is built around a set of paired stories, one from the Qur'an or authentic traditions, and one related modern story. The overall objectives are: (1) to awaken the children's awareness of their identity and worth as Muslims, (2) to model Islamic behavior patterns, and (3) to cultivate a sense of identification and community with Muslims of long ago and in other parts of the modern world. While the unit is designed for kindergarten, its stories and activities may be useful for values instruction throughout the primary grades in a variety of instructional settings, including full-time, weekend and home schools. This unit, emphasizing values education, may also be useful in Muslim parenting classes.

Each lesson consists of the story pair, to be presented to the children orally or dramatically, and suggested discussion guidelines and activities through which the values and related behaviors are developed and reinforced in the children's understanding.

The 15 lessons are intended to implement teaching objectives in various units taught in a typical Islamic kindergarten social studies curriculum, on a selective or exhaustive basis, throughout the year.

1. Allah

The child will understand that:

- Allah created all things (i.e., all things come from Allah.
- Allah loves those who believe in Him.
- Allah rewards and punishes people based on their behavior.
- Allah sees us wherever we are, whatever we do.

2. Worship

The child will learn that:

- Muslims worship Allah in several ways (five pillars).
- Children can participate in Islamic worship.
- Worshipping Allah is positive and rewarded.

3. Self-identity as a Muslim

The child will learn that:

In actions by oneself, toward oneself:

- Muslims obey Allah's commands.
- Muslims practice many good deeds.
- Muslims try to be patient.
- Muslims love to learn.
- Muslims keep themselves clean.
- Muslims eat healthy food and avoid forbidden foods.
- Muslims protect themselves from danger.

In interpersonal relations (family, friends, environment).

- Muslims obey parents and treat them with respect.
- All Muslims are like brothers and sisters.

- Muslims are kind and generous to others.
- Muslims share what they have with others.
- Muslims treat older people with special respect.
- Muslims help and serve others.
- Muslims tell the truth.
- Muslims speak kindly and politely so others feel good.
- Muslims are brave and pray to Allah for strength.
- Muslims are kind to animals.
- Muslims keep their environment clean and safe.

4. Developing a sense of history and tradition:

The child will learn that:

- The Prophets lived long ago.
- Prophets and Sahaba are models for our behavior.
- People long ago lived differently from us now (houses, clothing, transportation, things they used in everyday life).
- People long ago had the same feelings as we do now.
- Muslims long ago practiced Islam just as we do.
- People in different countries speak different languages.
- Now and long ago, some people believe in Allah, and some do not.
- Muslims then and now celebrate 'Id festivals together.

Each story in this *Modern Storybook* is one of a pair. Each pair, together with the teaching suggestions, constitutes a lesson for implementation of a curriculum of Islamic values education. The overall objective of the unit is that the child identify him- or herself as a Muslim in conjunction with identifying the values and behaviors appropriate to Muslim social life.

For use in full-time schools, it is essential to emphasize that the lessons in this unit are not to be completed in one piece. They are intended for use from time to time throughout the kindergarten year. The lessons may be used in groups or individually as a resource for implementing other units in the curriculum, such as "Personal Social Development," "Family" and "My Community."[1] [See Index for typical kindergarten study topics covered in the stories.] It is also not essential that the lessons be completed in the sequence presented here, except where specifically noted in the teaching suggestions. The same applies to use in weekend schools, where the stories may complement Islamic studies or other programs.

The mode of implementation involves three phases. First, each story is intended to be read or told to children in the home setting, or in group settings such as classrooms or weekend schools. Second, discussion of the story by the children is essential, so it is strongly recommended that adequate time and preparation be allowed for comprehension and development of the concepts and ideas contained in each story pair. Third, followup activities may also accompany each pair of stories to complete the learning experience.

The following paragraphs describe the lesson materials, define their goals and objectives and discuss their use in the home or classroom.

STORY A: THE HISTORICAL, AUTHENTIC STORY

The first story in each pair consists of an incident mentioned in the Qur'an or in one of the major collections of Hadith. The feature which they all have in common is that young children are the actors in these stories. Either the story in these important Islamic sources is told about a young child, or the narrator is the child in the story. Thus we are not explaining to the child how children were treated or how they were acted upon, but we are giving children a direct link to the excellent example of young children as Muslims.

The authentic stories have several objectives. First, they are to illustrate important Islamic beliefs and values through the actions of some Prophets and Sahaba when they were children. As an introduction to thinking about history and tradition, modern children are given a taste of the way these early Muslims lived long ago. They are given a sense of the achievements of children, and a model of excellent behavior. They are shown how children contributed to the community of believers in important ways.

These authentic stories have been retold in simple vocabulary and syntax. Since children respond well to direct dialog, it has been employed extensively, but it is important to note that these are not direct translations of the Arabic dialog, even where such is quoted in the Qur'an or Hadith. This diversion has been necessary in order to make the language in these stories accessible to young children. In spite of this compromise, every attempt has been made to adhere to the original ideas, and in each case, the original source has been cited exactly for reference by the adult reader. The English translations upon which the stories are based on Yusuf Ali's rendering of the meaning of the Holy Qur'an and M. Khan's

---

[1] These unit titles are taken from the *Iqra Curriculum: Kindergarten*, Iqra International Education Foundation, Chicago, 1991.

translation of Sahih Al-Bukhari, unless another source has been specifically cited. The author has also referred to the original Arabic in preparing the stories. The teacher or parent should prepare for the lesson by reading the original passage in the Qur'an or Hadith whenever possible. And the truth resides with Allah, subhanahu wa ta'ala.

STORY B: THE MODERN STORY

The second story in each pair presents a story featuring modern children in familiar situations. The story's central idea is drawn from one or more of the beliefs or values contained in the authentic vignette. Some present a direct parallel, while others illustrate only one or more aspects of the first story. Some are more loosely associated with the first story.

The purpose of the modern story is to relate the ideas and values in the first, historical incident to the lives and situations of modern children in various parts of the world. It is intended to help the children appreciate the lives of the Prophets and their companions by creating parallels and connections with familiar situations in their own lives. It is intended to help the children learn to apply Islamic beliefs and values to their own understanding and behavior by framing them in familiar terms. The children may compare and contrast their own lives with those of earlier people by way of developing a sense of history and tradition.

To help teachers with preparation, pre-reading activities, discussion guidelines and supplementary activities have been described in detail for each story. The lesson plans are printed after each story pair.

These lesson plans and teaching ideas are organized for ease of use. The following features will aid in determining when and how to implement the stories in the course of a busy year:

1. Activities, listed separately for each story, are printed after each story pair. They constitute one lesson featuring an authentic and a modern story. Lesson concepts are crossreferenced when appropriate, together with associated children's literature selections.

2. An index of lesson topics covered and unit titles with which the stories may be used is provided at the end of the teacher's notes. This information is repeated at the beginning of each lesson.

3. Lesson plans are divided into four levels of discussion and activities, as described below.

USING THE TEACHING SUGGESTIONS WITH THE STORIES

The stories are to be read to the children, told to them with interaction by the teacher, or presented dramatically. Following each story, the storyteller should engage the child or children in talking about it. The discussion guidelines and activities which are suggested for use with the *Modern Storybook* envision three levels of discussion/activity for each pair of stories.

- **Pre-reading Activity** is intended to familiarize the children with new vocabulary, to set the scene for the story and arouse their curiosity and anticipation.

- **Level I (Comprehension)** is intended to help clarify and expand the ideas contained in the stories, some of which may be new to the children.

- **Level II (Analysis and Value Building)** is intended to help identify and develop the values portrayed in the stories and help the children learn to apply them in their lives.

- **Level III (Reinforcement, Enrichment and Evaluation Activities)** is intended to help reinforce specific behaviors discussed in the stories and develop the skills associated with these behaviors. Some activities are intended as bridge or springboard activities to other disciplines, or as knowledge enhancement. Others serve as evaluation tools.

It is expected that the teacher will select those discussion points and activities which are feasible for the particular group size and composition, and adapt them based on his or her knowledge of the children. Particular emphasis should be placed at the outset of discussion upon comprehension of possibly unfamiliar words or concepts. Let the children lead in asking, or anticipate their questions.

After discussing for comprehension, the discussion may move to second level-questions, such as "why," "how," "what if," etc. For each story, a number of values have been identified in the teacher's notes which proceed from the characters' actions and the situation. The goal of the discussion is to analyze in simple terms the character's motivation and actions to determine why he or she acted in a certain way, and what is important about those actions for us as Muslims.

The stories may admit of varied interpretations which will develop from group discussion. This is very desirable, since it stimulates individual contributions and cooperative thought by the group. The teacher must balance the roles of leader, guide and facilitator. Allowing the students to draw their own conclusions supports retention of the ideas and values.

The third stage of discussion and activity involves modeling and reinforcing the values and behaviors identified in the stories. Role-play and constructive and functional activities are suggested to accompany each pair of stories, as well as enrichment activities to broaden and integrate the learning experience. Some of the activities are useful evaluation tools.

This index will help in selecting lessons from this unit to supplement objectives from regular Kindergarten teaching units and lessons across the curriculum, and aid in coordinating Islamic values lessons from this unit with lesson plans in a variety of disciplines throughout the year. The categories refer to concepts covered in the stories and/or teaching suggestions.

TOPIC: LESSON NUMBERS (#)

Animals: #1, #13

Assertiveness: #11, #12

Belief in Allah: #1, #2, #3, #5

Body Parts: #10

Celebration of 'Id: #4b, #8b

Charity: #2, #6, #8b, #13(to animals), #14b, #15

Cleanliness: #2b, #9, #10b, #11b

Community Helpers: #6, #13, #11b, #14

Courage: #2, #4 (on Hajj), #12, #14

Creation: #1

Defending Islam: #14

Environment: #1, #8b (recycling), #11, #13

Family: #2, #3, #4, #5, #6, #8, #12, #14

Fear and Bravery: #2, #3, #4b, #11, #14

Food and Nutrition: #7, #9, #10

Gifts and Giving: #8, #15

Guests: #6, #10, #15

Hajj (Pilgrimage): #4

Halal and Haram: #2, #3, #7, #8 (toys)

Health: #7, #10

Helping at Home: #2b, #3, #5, #6

History (life long ago): #1, #2, #4, #5, #8, #9, #11, #14, #15

Honesty: #2b, #11

Kindness: #2, #3, #5B, #6, #8b, #9, #10, #11b, #13, #15

Learning (Qur'an and other subjects): #1, #4, #5, #6, #12

Manners: #3, #6, #9, #10, #12, #15

Part II:

The Modern Storybook and Teaching Suggestions

وَجَٰهِدُوا۟ فِى ٱللَّهِ حَقَّ جِهَادِهِۦ هُوَ ٱجْتَبَىٰكُمْ وَمَا جَعَلَ
عَلَيْكُمْ فِى ٱلدِّينِ مِنْ حَرَجٍ مِّلَّةَ أَبِيكُمْ إِبْرَٰهِيمَ هُوَ سَمَّىٰكُمُ
ٱلْمُسْلِمِينَ مِن قَبْلُ وَفِى هَٰذَا لِيَكُونَ ٱلرَّسُولُ شَهِيدًا عَلَيْكُمْ
وَتَكُونُوا۟ شُهَدَآءَ عَلَى ٱلنَّاسِ فَأَقِيمُوا۟ ٱلصَّلَوٰةَ وَءَاتُوا۟ ٱلزَّكَوٰةَ
وَٱعْتَصِمُوا۟ بِٱللَّهِ هُوَ مَوْلَىٰكُمْ فَنِعْمَ ٱلْمَوْلَىٰ وَنِعْمَ ٱلنَّصِيرُ

And strive for Allah with the endeavor which is His right.
He has chosen you and has not laid upon you any hardship in religion.
The faith of your father Abraham is yours.
He has named you Muslims of old times and in this (Scripture),
That the messenger may be a witness against you,
And that you may be a witness against mankind.
So establish worship, pay the poor-due, and hold fast to Allah.
He is your Protecting Friend. A blessed Patron and a blessed Helper!
(Qur'an 22:78)

I AM A MUSLIM

A MODERN STORYBOOK

Written by Susan Douglass
Illustrated by Carol Joumaa

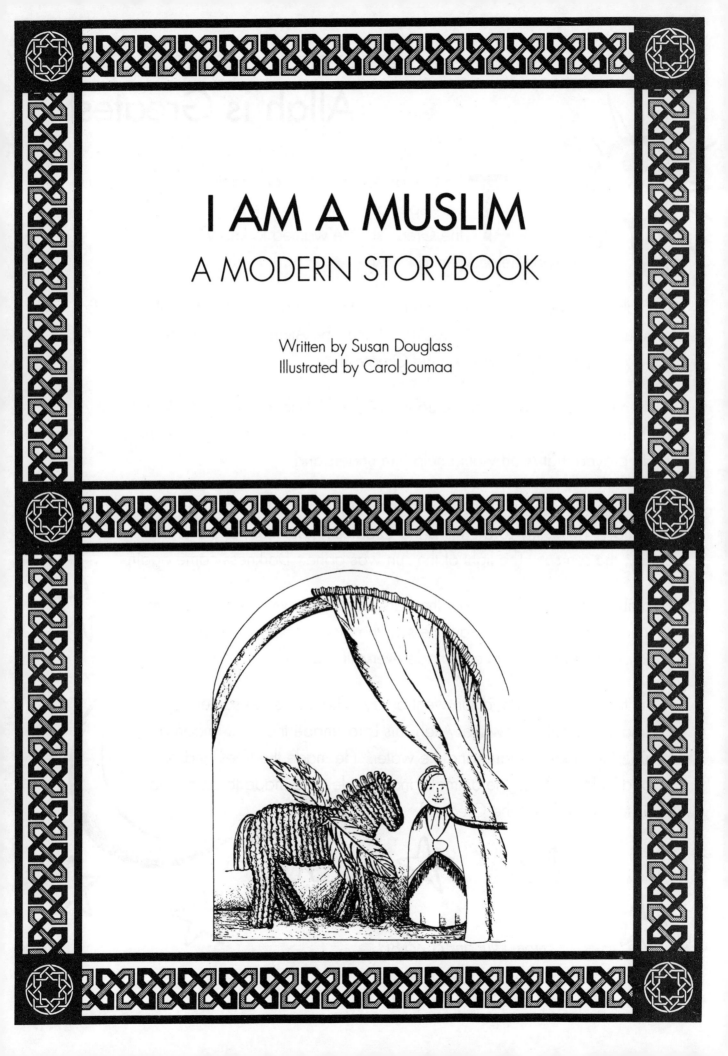

Allah is Greatest

The Qur'an tells the story of Ibrahim. Ibrahim was a very special young boy. He tried to know what is the Greatest. He wanted to know his Lord, Allah. Allah helped him to know.

Ibrahim looked up at the sky one night. He saw a beautiful star shining. He thought that it must be the Greatest. It must be Allah. But then, the star went out of sight. That couldn't be the Greatest!

Then he saw the moon come up in the sky. A bright, shining circle in the sky! "This is my Lord." But then the moon set into the shadows, just like the star. He prayed that Allah would help him understand.

Then he saw the sun rise. The brightest light, like a fire lighting up the whole world! "This is my Lord! This is the Greatest!" But then, at the end of the day, the sun set. The light of the sun was gone. Darkness came again.

Ibrahim understood. He saw the stars and the moon. He saw how they lit up the dark night. He saw the sun, the biggest thing in the sky. Sunshine made it warm and made everything grow.

But the stars, moon and sun went away. There must be something greater. Ibrahim knew that Allah, his Lord, made the stars, moon and sun. He made the land and the water. He made the trees and our food. He made all the animals and people. He made Ibrahim and his family. Allah is the Greatest!

From Qur'an, 6:76-80

Who Made All Things?

I like to lie down on my back in the cool grass. I can look up into the sky. Sometimes it is blue, and it looks so big. Sometimes I see white clouds up there. They move and grow fatter and fatter. Sometimes the whole sky is white and gray. The rain starts to fall on my face. In the winter, snow falls from the sky. I like to taste it. Where did the sky come from? The One who made this must surely be the Greatest!

There is a big tree in our backyard. It has brown roots like big fingers that go into the ground. What's down there? If I get on my hands and knees and put my face close to the ground, I see things moving. I see little ants going down into a hole. I see a caterpillar on the ground. A tiny spider is climbing up the tree bark. I follow the trunk up, up with my eyes. There is a squirrel sitting on the branch. He swishes his tail at me. He's not scared of me, because I'm way down here. Up at the top of the tree are so many leaves. It's like a big umbrella with holes in it. The sun shines through. I have to squint my eyes. How did this tree get here? Where do all the bugs and animals come from? The One who made these must surely be the Greatest!

We have a garden. We got some packs of seeds from the store. We dug up the ground with a shovel.

We broke up all the lumps of dirt. I like to crumble it with my hands. I like the way it smells. We put the seeds in the ground in rows. Now, little green sprouts are coming out of the ground. I remember last summer. The little leaves turned into big plants. Then flowers came out of the leaves. Then they grew round, red tomatoes. We pulled long, orange carrots out of the mud. We washed them and ate them. They were so good! How did those things grow so big? The One who made them must surely be the Greatest!

When I'm tired at night, I like to sit with my mother and father. They talk to me. We read books. When I ask them about things, they know answers. They tell me stories. Our baby is sitting on Mama's lap. She is not crying. She wants to play with me. She has a beautiful face, and little fingers. She laughs at the faces I make at her. She wiggles her tiny toes when I touch them. It feels nice to sit with my family.

It's time to go to bed. The house is almost quiet. The lights are off. It's dark, and it's warm in my bed. I hear small sounds outside. From the window I can see the shadows of daytime things. The house, the tree, and the garden. The moon and some stars hang in the sky. How did night come? How did we get here? The One who made the quiet, dark night must surely be the Greatest!

Who made all these? And who made me? Allah is the One! He is the Greatest!

LESSON PLAN 1, STORY A: Allah is Greatest

TOPICS: Belief in Allah, Creation, Animals, Nature, Environment, Worship, History, *Tawhid*

PRE-READING ACTIVITY

1. Talk about the Qur'an as a book from Allah; discuss its contents as being about Allah, about how Muslims should act, and also as a book of stories about Prophets and people long ago.

2. Identify Ibrahim as the Father of the Prophets, who lived long ago in a place near a river. You may wish to locate Mesopotamia on a globe.

LEVEL I (COMPREHENSION)

1. Explain that Ibrahim was just like any person who wonders where the world came from and who made it, but that he was also a Prophet. Define the term "prophet," explaining that Allah sent people to explain about Allah and about what is good for people. Allah gave them knowledge and understanding to tell other people. He taught them how to worship Allah so they could teach others. [For more on this topic, see Lesson #4 , "Young Muslims Worship Allah."]

2. Discuss the three words for God in the story: Allah, the Greatest, Lord. One is the name, one means that nothing is above or more important than "the Greatest"; one refers to the quality of being over all things as the One who controls everything else.

3. Ask the children to tell what Ibrahim saw first, and what happened to it; then second, then third.

LEVEL II (ANALYSIS AND VALUE BUILDING)

1. Ask if the children have ever asked Allah for something. Elicit responses on what they ask for. Tell them that Ibrahim asked Allah to help him have knowledge, to be sure about what Allah is.

2. Discuss the idea of things "going away," or "dying" or "changing into something else." Talk about how this happens to everything in the world, asking for examples of living things which change, die or go away; about seasons changing; about sun, earth, moon and stars moving and going out of sight; about people being born and dying. Elicit examples from the children's experience of such phenomena.

3. Ask the children who made things change, who made things come and go. Allah! He is the only One who never changes, never dies and never goes. That is what Ibrahim understood. Explain that he tried to teach his people this lesson about Allah.

LEVEL III (REINFORCEMENT, ENRICHMENT AND EVALUATION ACTIVITIES)

1. Bring examples of changing, growing or dying things into the class, or pictures of stars and planets.

2. Recite the poem from the Iqra' Kindergarten curriculum, "I am a Muslim and Allah made me!" in Unit 2.

LESSON PLAN 1, STORY B: Who Made All Things?

TOPICS: Belief in Allah, Creation, Animals, Nature, Environment, Worship, History, *Tawhid*

This story is intended to place Ibrahim's experience in a familiar context for children. Discussion, and activities attempt to draw the children in the group into this experience, and also to encourage the experience of reflection and observation when alone or with friends, and to cultivate emotional response to natural beauty, which is so often neglected in a busy, urban environment.

PRE-READING

1.   Talk with the children about quiet time alone and about thinking, like talking with themselves. Try to elicit children's responses about what they think about when alone in a nice place. Discuss nice places where they like to be alone. What do they like to do? (read, walk, play make-believe, draw, etc.)

LEVEL I (COMPREHENSION)/ LEVEL II (ANALYSIS AND VALUE BUILDING)

1.   Talk about being outdoors and looking at the things Allah made. Elicit the children's recollection of seeing things mentioned in the story, such as looking at the sky, sitting in or under a tree, having a flower or vegetable garden, the time of day when the family sits together, and their experiences when going to bed at night, falling asleep or other nighttime adventures.

2.   How do we feel when we are alone in a beautiful place? Draw the children's attention to the multitude of created things — great and small: the weather, the sky, the whole earth and the universe. [The following activities serve as an answer to this question, and the teacher may bring up the question of feelings with regard to verbal and artistic expression.]

LEVEL III (REINFORCEMENT, ENRICHMENT AND EVALUATION ACTIVITIES)

1.   Show photographs from a nature calendars to show the variety of scenery. Talk about the feelings each picture expresses.

2.   Take the children out for a nature walk, noticing large and small things. [Disciplinary crossover — combine with science activities of observation.] Discuss how Allah created everything perfectly and with beauty.

3.   Have the children go out and look at the sky in any weather.

   a.   Ask the children to describe what they see

   b.   Do shaving cream paintings on light blue paper.

   c.   Write a poem about the sky with the teacher, or read sky poems.

4.   Have the children draw a picture of their favorite place.

The Idols

Ibrahim's family and their friends didn't believe in Allah. They didn't know what Allah helped Ibrahim to understand. They used to pray to idols. They had some that were shaped like animals. They had some shaped like people. Some looked like monsters. The idols were made of clay, wood, stone or metal.

They believed that these idols helped them. They thought the idols could make it rain or make the sun shine. If they were sick, they asked the idols to make them well. Sometimes they put food and drinks in front of them.

Ibrahim told the people to believe in Allah. He told them Allah is the greatest. He told them that Allah created everything. He told them to stop praying to idols. He told the people they were wrong.

Those people got very angry at Ibrahim. He was a young boy telling them what to do. He said, "I believe Allah is the greatest. You will see that you are wrong."

When the people went away, Ibrahim went to the idols and broke them. He did not break the biggest one.

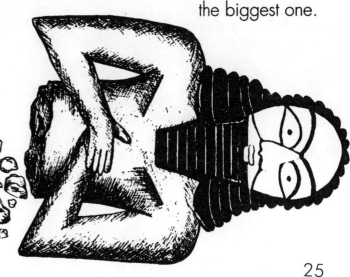

The people called that one the chief idol.

The people saw their idols broken. They were angry and scared. They brought Ibrahim and asked him, "Who did this to our gods?"

Ibrahim was very smart. He said, "The chief idol did it. Ask the idols, if they can talk."

They answered, "You know they cannot talk!"

So Ibrahim asked, "Why do you pray to something that can't talk or even help itself?" "You pray to these instead of Allah. But they can't help you or hurt you."

But the people didn't like to hear that they were wrong. They tried to burn Ibrahim. But Allah saved him from their fire.

From Qur'an, 21:51-71

Guess What?

AFTER READING EACH OF THE NEXT FIVE STORIES, MAKE UP YOUR OWN ENDING. HOW DO THE PEOPLE IN THE STORY SOLVE THEIR PROBLEM? THEN, READ THE ENDING WHICH IS PRINTED UPSIDE DOWN AFTER THE STORY, AND SEE HOW IT IS DIFFERENT FROM YOUR ENDING.

Two Brothers

Once there were two brothers. They had fun playing together. The trouble was, just when they were having the most fun, they started to fight. One of them found a nice toy. The smaller brother found a great car, and he knew how to make great car sounds. It looked like so much fun that his older brother wanted to try it, too! So he reached out and took that car away from his little brother. And what did that little brother do? Well, he started to yell and scream and cry. And then he grabbed that car back, and the other brother pulled it harder.

And they both yelled, "No, I want it!"

And then it wasn't fun anymore. Then, they were angry.

Then, their mother and father heard them fighting. They were angry, too.

They said, "Why don't you share the toys with your brother?"

But all they both could say was, "No, I want it!"

Can you guess what happened?

Alternative ending:

Then, the toy car flew out of their hands. It fell on the floor and broke. Now the brothers could not play with it. They felt very sorry for not taking turns. They should have shared it.

The brothers picked up the pieces of the car and went to their mother and father. "We're sorry we didn't share. We're sorry we fought and yelled. Would you please help us fix the broken car? Then we promise to share it."

Father looked at the car. He said, "I might be able to fix it with glue. But now you see what happens when you fight. Go and get me the glue."

When the car was fixed, Father put it on the shelf. "Now the car won't break again, in sha' Allah."

"As long as you remember to take turns and not to fight," said Mother.

"We'll remember, in sha' Allah," said the brothers.

The next day, they took the car off the shelf. It was almost as good as new. This is how they shared the car: each one sat on one side of the long hallway. Then they took turns rolling the car to each other, catching it and racing it back very fast. Soon they were laughing and having lots of fun!

Two Sisters

Once there were two sisters. They liked to play tea party. They liked to make clay cookies. Their mother saw them playing tea party. She had an idea. She brought them some juice and a cake. She let them put the juice in their tea cups. She put the cake on a dish and let them cut it.

She said, "Say Bismillah and share the cake."

But the big sister said, "Let me cut it." She cut a very big piece. And she started to eat.

The small sister said, "Give me some, too."

"All right." But there was only a little piece left. She put it on her sister's dish.

"Why did you give me a little piece? I want more! I want a big piece!" But there was none left.

Can you guess what happened?

_____

Alternative ending:

The older sister looked at her plate. She took the fork and cut a piece off of her cake. She put it on her younger sister's dish. "Now we have the same amount of cake," she said. "I'm sorry I didn't cut it right the first time."

"Thank you," said the younger sister.

Mother said, "Muslims should share the good things Allah gives them. If you want something good for yourself, you should want others to have good things, too. Prophet Muhammad taught us that this is important for Muslims."

Two Friends

Hassan and Abdullah were friends. They liked to visit each other's houses. They went to the playground. They climbed trees together. They had picnics. One day, Abdullah pulled a nice toy out of his pocket. It was a robot. It had moving arms and legs. It had a light. And it buzzed loudly when it walked.

"Look what I have!" said Abdullah. "Let's play with it."

"Look how it goes, it's a space robot!" said Hassan.

Then Abdullah's mother called him. He said, "Wait a minute, my mother wants me. I'll be right back."

Hassan put the robot in his own pocket. "I want that!" he thought. He hoped Abdullah forgot about it. Hassan took it home. But it wasn't his.

When Abdullah came back, his friend was not there. His toy was not there. Abdullah was very sad.

Can you guess what happened?

Alternative Ending:

Hassan played with the robot for a while at home. Then he remembered his friend Abdullah. Hassan wanted to play ball with Abdullah. He started to feel badly for taking the robot. Hassan thought, "How can I go to his house and ask him to play after I took his toy? He might be sad."

Then Hassan got an idea. He went to ask his Mother what to do. She said, "Hassan, you know that it was wrong to take Abdullah's toy. Now, you should take the robot back and tell the truth. Tell Abdullah that you're sorry."

Hassan took the robot and went to his friend's house. He knocked on the door.

"Salamu 'alaikum!" said Abdullah.

"Wa 'alaikum As-salam!" replied Hassan. "I brought back your robot. I'm sorry I took it. Let's play outside together."

"I'm glad you came back," said Abdullah. "If you want to borrow the robot, just ask me next time."

"Thanks," said Hassan. "Let's go out to play!"

A Family

Once there was a family. Everyone in the house was very busy. The children played. Father was fixing things with his tools. Mother was making bread. When they were all finished, the house was a mess. There were toys all over the house. There were tools all over. There was flour and dough all over the kitchen.

Mother said to one child, "Please help me clean up the kitchen."

The child didn't move. "But I want to eat bread."

Father said to the other children, "There, it's all fixed! Please pick up your toys and help me clean up with this broom."

But the children said, "We want to play. It's too hard to sweep up all that mess." And they kept right on playing.

Can you guess what happened?

Alternative Ending:

Father and Mother met in the kitchen. "The children don't want to help. It's too hard to do all of this work by ourselves. What can we do?"

Father had an idea. "We could make a game out of it. Everyone gets a little job. The first one to finish his job will have a surprise."

"Good idea," said Mother, "Let's call the children."

Everyone came to the kitchen. Mother had brooms, rags and sponges. Father had boxes and the vacuum cleaner. "Let's see who can help clean up and finish the work first. The smallest ones can help pick up the toys. One of you can take this box to help me put my tools away."

"Who can clean the table with the sponges?" said Mother. "Who can sweep the flour from the floor?"

Soon, everyone had a job. The children even thought it was fun, since the whole family worked together. They worked so well that everyone finished at the same time! So they all got a surprise. Father brought out a box of ice cream and the family sat together to have a treat in the clean house.

Prefer Time

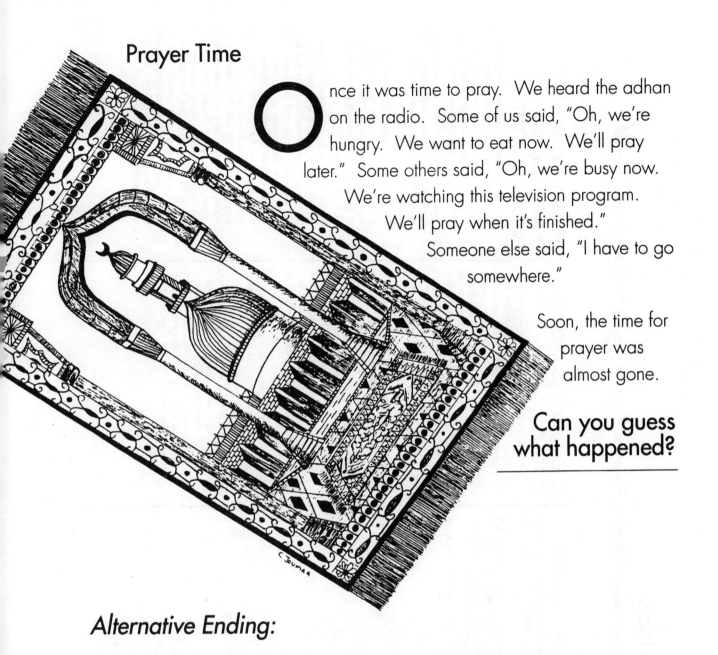

Once it was time to pray. We heard the adhan on the radio. Some of us said, "Oh, we're hungry. We want to eat now. We'll pray later." Some others said, "Oh, we're busy now. We're watching this television program. We'll pray when it's finished."

Someone else said, "I have to go somewhere."

Soon, the time for prayer was almost gone.

Can you guess what happened?

Alternative Ending:

When we stop to listen, a small voice inside us reminds us when we forget. The voice reminds us of Allah. We remember how Allah gave us and our families life. He gives us the power to play and have fun. Allah gives us food and water, sunshine and rain. He gives us houses and everything we use.

Allah taught Prophet Muhammad to pray five times a day. Prophet Muhammad was our teacher. It is not difficult to pray. It does not take much time. After prayer, we feel very good. It feels good to obey Allah.

All the people in this story remembered Allah. They left what they were doing and washed themselves for prayer. They finished their prayers before the time was gone.

LESSON PLAN 2, STORY A The Idols

TOPICS: Belief in Allah, Worship, Halal and Haram, Parents, Obeying, Politeness, Kindness, Respect for Elders, History, *Tawhid*

PRE-READING ACTIVITY

1. Get several art books which show ancient Mesopotamian idols and/or those of other cultures, both ancient and modern. Discuss ones that are made to look good or bad, frightening or funny. Explain how people worshipped these in Ibrahim's time, before him and even now. Tell how the images were/are carried, offerings are made, music and dances are done in front of them.

2. Talk about how images of various kinds make people laugh, or be frightened or feel good or bad, such as cartoon shows, or scary pictures or masks. Elicit the children's recollections of such experiences. Explain that people believed that these pictures or statues could help them in the ways mentioned in the story.

LEVEL I (COMPREHENSION)

1. Ask the children to recall what Ibrahim told the people who believed these idols had powers.

2. Ask the children to relate how Ibrahim played a trick on the idols to show the people that the idols had no power. Recall the details to the children if necessary.

3. Recall Lesson #1, asking what Ibrahim knew about Allah.

LEVEL II (ANALYSIS AND VALUE BUILDING)

1. Explain that Ibrahim was a young boy talking to older people, telling them that they were wrong. Engage the group in discussion about whether or not a young person should do this. Discuss the people's anger at Ibrahim. Do we like to be told we are wrong? Ask the children how they feel when someone tells them they are wrong.

2. Introduce the idea of worship. The sequence of ideas might go something like this:

   If we know that Allah is the Greatest, and he made us and everything for us, we must thank Him. That is a kind of worship. If we know Allah is the only One who can help us and keep us from harm, then we must ask Him to help us and give us what we need. That is also a kind of worship. Saying that we believe in Allah, that He is the Greatest, and thanking and asking are what we do in prayer.

   Ibrahim told the people to stop worshipping pieces of stone. He told them to worship Allah.

3. It might be possible with some groups to talk about how worshipping idols doesn't always mean praying to stones. It can mean being selfish, like wanting to have things and forgetting the feelings or needs of others. The story "I Want it" illustrates these ideas.

LEVEL III (REINFORCEMENT, ENRICHMENT AND EVALUATION ACTIVITIES)

1. See #1, above, under Prereading Activity, for showing pictures of idols from various cultures. One might also discuss images the children may have seen of Christian saints, of Maryam or Issa, 'alaihuma salaam.

2. Read from Muslim Nursery Rhymes (Islamic Foundation Publications) appropriate poems to reinforce the idea of worship and obedience to Allah.

3. Combine with Islamic studies lessons on the meaning of prayer, how to pray, how to make wudu, the motions of prayer, assembly in lines, etc. The group may pray together as a concluding activity.

4. Shape play-dough into animal or people shapes in front of and with the children. Discuss with them how clear it is that people make such things, and that these forms don't have the power to do anything. Compare these to dolls and stuffed toys, discussing how the children make them move, give them voices, etc., as pretend play. Contrast this with the creatures to whom Allah gives life and movement and voices and a spirit. Discuss the idol pictures again, explaining how ignorant people made these things and then prayed to them, even though they clearly had no power. Compare this with pretending, saying that people sometimes forgot that they were pretending at the beginning.

LESSON PLAN 2, STORY B Guess What?

TOPICS: Belief in Allah, Worship, Halal and Haram, Parents, Obeying, Politeness, Kindness, Charity, Cleanliness, Respect for Elders, Stealing, Sharing, Serving Others, Telling the Truth, Toys, Time and Schedules, Science.

This story is about loving things more than people and more than Allah, about wanting things and not being kind to mother and father, siblings and other people, and about thinking that things will give us more than obeying Allah by being kind, considerate and helpful in a timely way. There are four situations presented, and they are best dealt with singly, with discussion and activities following each.

PRE-READING ACTIVITY

1. Explain that these stories are about what happens when something goes wrong. Explain that the children must find out what is wrong in the story, then find out how to make it turn out right. Tell them that the story is only partly finished, and they must make an ending for it.

LEVEL I (COMPREHENSION)/ LEVEL II (ANALYSIS AND VALUE BUILDING)

1. Ask the children what happened to the characters. Ask how each character felt.

2. Let the children describe a time they got in trouble, and their parents or siblings were angry. Discuss their feelings and draw out ideas about the probable feelings of others in the situation they described.

3. For the first two situations, discuss sharing toys and sharing food. Why is it good or not good to share. How can it be done? (taking turns, playing with similar toys like cars together, dividing a cookie or other treat equally, or not eating in front of others if there is not enough to share) Elicit the children's suggestions of ways to share toys and food.

4. Discuss ideas of what belongs to oneself and to others, and what does that mean. Discuss attendant feelings.

5. Talk about helping, what it means to help at home or in school. What jobs always need to be done at home, such as cleaning or picking up. Who usually does that work at each child's home? What jobs does each child have at home? What about older siblings? Discuss the children's feelings about helping, whether it is fun or not, and how they feel when they do a good job, or do something to help without being asked. Talk about how people feel when no one helps them with work. [See Activity #2, below — The Little Red Hen.] Finally, discuss what would happen if families didn't help each other with work, or if no one took care of these jobs at home. Discuss the benefits of

helping, cooperation, and tell how Prophet Muhammad (S) did work at home and helped his wives and children

6. Introduce the idea of schedules, missing the school bus or other appointment. Explain that Allah has a schedule for every Muslim to worship Him each day. He gave this schedule to Prophet Muhammad, who taught it to us. [See activities #3 and #4 below, and Worksheet #1.]

LEVEL III (REINFORCEMENT, ENRICHMENT AND EVALUATION ACTIVITIES)

1. Role play the situations described. Have the children act out what the children in each situation should do, how they should behave.

2. Read other stories about stealing, sharing, etc. from Aesop or Berenstain Bears. Read The Little Red Hen or similar story. Discuss good and bad behavior by the characters, and the character's feelings at various points in the stories.

3. Have dramatic play about missing a bus, being late for something, missing something because of time. Relate this to Allah's schedule for Muslim prayers. Have children pray together the noontime prayer.

4. This story may also be used in conjunction with activities about time and schedules, and relating these to the Muslim's daily prayer schedule. [See also, Lesson Plan #5B, Level III, Activity #9 for alternative placement.] You may combine this activity with beginning to teach the prayer times in Islamic studies, combined with a science activity about the sun, the earth and its daily movement. See following activity.

5. Color Worksheet #1, "When Do Muslims Pray?" As a preliminary activity and science crossover—try to observe the changing position of the sun on several days upon coming to school, at lunchtime, and at the end of the school day. It might help to draw a picture of its position using a familiar landmark, or to take polaroid pictures of the sun's relative position from the same spot.

LESSON PLAN 2, STORY B Guess What?

TOPICS: Belief in Allah, Worship, Halal and Haram, Parents, Obeying, Politeness, Kindness, Charity, Cleanliness, Respect for Elders, Stealing, Sharing, Serving Others, Telling the Truth, Toys, Time and Schedules, Science.

6. After each story, have the group make up alternative endings or continuations for the story—"What happened next?" "How does this story end?" The results may be written on a flip chart or on the blackboard. As a final activity for each story, compare the class' endings with those printed upside down at the end of the stories.

When Do Muslims Pray?

Fajr	Color the sky pink.
Zuhr	Color the sky blue and the sun yellow.
Asr	Color the sky blue and the sun yellow.
Maghrib	Color the sky orange.
Isha'	Color the stars and moon silver. Color the sky black

Ibrahim's Father

brahim's father was named Azar. Ibrahim loved him and wanted to help him. He was an idol-maker. He also believed that the idols could help people or hurt them. Azar worshipped the idols.

Ibrahim asked his father, "Why do you worship idols? They can't see, they can't make themselves. They can't help you or hurt you."

His father was angry. Ibrahim said, "Believe in Allah. I know something that you don't know. Allah helped me to understand. Don't follow the Satan! I don't want Allah to punish you."

Ibrahim's father was so angry that he forgot himself. He told Ibrahim, "You don't believe in my gods?" He said, "I will stone you if you don't stop talking about Allah!" Ibrahim's father told him, "Go away from me for a long time!"

Was Ibrahim angry at his father? Did he try to hit him or say angry words back? No, Ibrahim was very sad. He wanted his father to believe in Allah. He wanted him to go to Paradise. Ibrahim asked Allah to forgive his father. He remembered his father's love and kindness when he was not angry.

From Qur'an, 6:75-80; 9:114; 19:41-48; 21:51-56; 26:77-86; 37:83- 99

Our Papa

Yusuf and Yassir were sitting in their room, each in a different corner. The door was shut tight. Papa shut it very hard. He was angry. He told them not to come out until they made peace.

Yusuf and Yassir were angry, too. They didn't think they should be stuck in their room.

"You got us in trouble, Yusuf," said Yassir.

"But you screamed at me!" answered Yusuf

"'Cause you took the ball away from me."

"Because you threw it at Mama's chair and hit her book."

"Humph!" humphed Yassir.

Yusuf and Yassir were silent. Yassir chewed on the string of his sweatshirt. Yusuf pulled at his socks until they were long and floppy.

"I don't like Papa when he gets mad," pouted Yusuf.

"He shouldn't shout and make his face all scary," joined Yassir.

"And he said some sharp words to us. Papa and Mama said that Allah doesn't like it when we say those things." said Yusuf.

"Allah will be angry with him, too. We're good," said Yusuf.

"They said Shaitan is with you when you get angry. So Papa shouldn't let Shaitan be with him."

"But Papa is always nice to us when we behave well," remembered Yusuf.

"Like when he takes us to the park sometimes." Yassir added.

"Remember when we got to ride in those boats?"

"And I caught that little fish and you almost fell in the water?" laughed Yassir.

"Yeah, and Papa held onto you and he almost fell in, too?"

"That was the most fun day. And we had a picnic," said Yassir.

"Maybe if we're good, Papa will take us on Saturday."

The two brothers were quiet again.

"Let's go tell Papa that we're sorry for fighting," said Yusuf.

"Let's tell him Allah will forgive him for getting angry at us. We'll ask Allah to forgive all of us," said Yassir.

LESSON PLAN 3 STORY A: Ibrahim's Father

Topics: Belief in Allah, Worship, Parents, Family, Halal and haram, Kindness, Manners, Poiliteness, Respect for Elders, History, *Tawhid*

PRE-READING ACTIVITY

1. Review the term "idol" and what some people have believed about them, using concepts from Lesson #2.

2. Introduce or review the context of Prophet Ibrahim's life and times long ago within the children's understanding.

LEVEL I (COMPREHENSION)

1. What job did Ibrahim's father do? (idolmaker) Discuss how Ibrahim reminded his father that the idols can't make themselves.

2. Discuss the way Ibrahim spoke to his father, how he told him that he was wrong.

3. Ask the children what Ibrahim's father said and did to Ibrahim.

4. What did Ibrahim do when his father became angry. (prayed for Allah to forgive him, remembered his father's kindness and love)

LEVEL II (ANALYSIS AND VALUE BUILDING).

1. Discuss why Ibrahim wanted his father to believe in Allah, since he loved him and didn't like to see him doing something wrong.

2. Why did his father become angry? Discuss the idea of a young person telling an older one that he or she is wrong. Discuss when it is all right to do so politely and when it is not good to tell our parents they are wrong, and especially when children speak loud and impolitely, which no one likes to hear. [This discussion is most useful when it develops from the children's opinions and ideas, though it might be somewhat difficult to facilitate. It might be least effective in the "telling" or preaching mode.]

3. Discuss what it means to "forget yourself" when you become angry. Ask what makes the children angry. Talk about the children's reactions of anger. Ask them how they express it. Discuss what ways are acceptable and what ways are not (harming others or oneself)

4. Build on I, #4 above, discussing how Ibrahim did not get angry at his father in return, but remembered his kindness and asked Allah to forgive him. He wanted only the good for him. This type of thinking is somewhat advanced for the children's short sense of perspective, but the goal here is to expose them to the idea.

LEVEL III (REINFORCEMENT, ENRICHMENT AND EVALUATION ACTIVITIES)

1. Roleplay situations that make the children angry (breaking a toy, losing something, not being allowed to do something, arguing with someone), with appropriate expressions of anger. Talk about other ways of diffusing anger than foot stamping, yelling, hitting, etc. (for example — running in place, counting to 10, looking for a favorite book, drawing a picture, singing a song)

2. Make masks on paper plates, depicting happy faces and angry faces. Tell a story in which the character becomes alternately angry and happy, having the children hold up first one mask, then the other to show the appropriate feeling.

3. Teach the children a du'a for parents, asking Allah for mercy on them. Have it photocopied, with the children making a decorative border using lace, edgings, glitter, and fancy collage materials.

LESSON PLAN 3, STORY B: Our Papa

TOPICS: Belief in Allah, Parents, Family, Kindness, Manners, Politeness, Respect for Elders, Obeying, Helping at Home.

PRE-READING ACTIVITY

1. Elicit the children's experiences of a time when they did something to make their father or mother angry. Have the children tell their stories briefly to the whole group, or break them up into groups and have them discuss among themselves and then choose one person to tell the whole group.

LEVEL I (COMPREHENSION)

1. Why were Yusuf and Yassir stuck in their room? Why was Papa angry? Let the children tell what they think happened to make Papa angry.

2. Were Yusuf and Yassir angry at each other, too?

3. How did Papa look when he was angry? (looked all red and scary) What did he do? (shout, shut the door hard, say sharp words)

4. What do Papa and Mama say about being angry and speaking sharp words? (Allah doesn't like it when we do that. Shaitan is with a person when he is angry.)

5. What did the boys remember about Papa when he was nice to them? When did they have the most fun day? (the trip to the park)

6. How did the boys make peace with each other? What did they want to say to Papa? (They said they were sorry for fighting. They asked Allah to forgive him for getting angry, and forgive them for fighting and making their Papa angry.)

LEVEL II (ANALYSIS AND VALUE BUILDING)

1. Discuss all of the things fathers do for us and the family. Make list using words and pictures.

2. Discuss all the ways fathers show that they love us, and how the children can show that they love their fathers.

3. Ask if children sometimes make mistakes or do things they shouldn't do. Why? (forgetting) Ask if parents ever make mistakes or forget. But parents still love children when they do wrong things, and children still love their parents. Most important, Allah forgives our mistakes when we are sorry and try to be better.

4. Introduce the idea (from Qur'an, S. Tauba, v. 71) in simple language that Muslims help each other to do good, and remind each other with kind words when they forget to do good. They help each other get to Paradise this way. They ask Allah to forgive mistakes.

5. Build on the idea in Story, II, #7, of how to gently, politely and kindly remind other people when they forget. Talk about families, and ask the children what they sometimes do to make their parents angry. Discuss again what Yusuf and Yassir did to make their father angry. Talk about how brothers and sisters can help keep peace in the family, (sharing, being kind and helping each other, helping parents) Explain that families love each other, remind each other and forgive each other even when they make mistakes.

LEVEL III (REINFORCEMENT, ENRICHMENT AND EVALUATION ACTIVITIES)

1. Have the children make a group list of all the nice things fathers do for us, then have the children draw a picture of the thing that they most enjoy doing with their father. Post these pictures together, or send them home with a message from the teacher.

2. Use puppets to dramatize for the children some incidents in which an adult makes a mistake in something mundane, like counting or naming colors, etc. and have the children practice politely correcting the "puppet adult." Use a pair of puppets to represent parent and child in a similar situation, but using a more serious mistake, such as forgetting to fasten a seat belt, or not recycling a bottle or can, etc., behaviors in which it is permissible for a child to remind or "correct" parents.

Young Muslims Worship Allah

When Prophet Muhammad ﷺ was alive, young boys and girls shared in Islamic worship with the older people. They had very important parts to play in the early days of Islam. Three companions told about being young Muslims then:

Sayid, son of Jubair, learned a large part of the Qur'an. He was ten years old when Prophet Muhammad ﷺ died. He started learning it when he was five or six years old.

Al-Sayid bin Yazid made Hajj with his parents. It was a very special Hajj journey. Prophet Muhammad ﷺ went with them. Al- Sayid was seven years old.

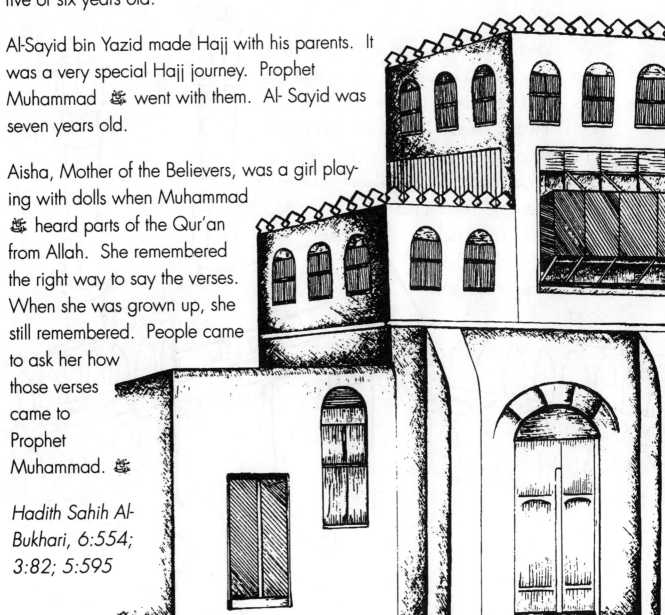

Aisha, Mother of the Believers, was a girl playing with dolls when Muhammad ﷺ heard parts of the Qur'an from Allah. She remembered the right way to say the verses. When she was grown up, she still remembered. People came to ask her how those verses came to Prophet Muhammad. ﷺ

Hadith Sahih Al-Bukhari, 6:554; 3:82; 5:595

Going on Hajj with My Family

June 1, 1992

Dear Diary,

Today Mom gave me a new outfit just for Hajj. It fits snuggly around my face and falls loosely to my waist. I have a new skirt to go with it. They are made of white cloth. I get to wear them when we go on the airplane tomorrow.

June 2, 1992

Dear Diary,

We landed in the big airport at Jedda. There were many, many people wearing clothes like ours. Then we rode on the bus for a few hours. I was so tired. The people kept chanting something in Arabic. I learned to say it, too, but I got tired. When we got to Mekka, it was prayer time. All the traffic stopped. I saw people pray right on the sidewalk. Daddy bought us lots of soda.

June 3, 1992

Dear Diary,

We went to the Holy Mosque where the Kaaba is. It is the biggest mosque I could ever imagine. I saw a big pile of shoes. I didn't want to lose my shoes in there. I felt people pushing and shoving all around me. It was crowded and hot when we walked around the Kaaba. There were lots people all around me. Daddy said I could ride on his shoulders. But I just held his hand very tight and walked around the Kaaba.

June 4, 1992

Dear Diary,

I don't think I'll get to see the black stone in the corner of the Kaaba. There are too many people. I got to run between two little hills today. The marble floor was cool but the air was hot. Long ago, Ibrahim's wife Haggar ran here on sand and rocks, looking for water for their baby. She would be surprised how easy it is now. Mom cut off a lock of my hair. I saw Daddy get all his hair cut off!

June 5, 1992

Dear Diary,

We slept in a tent instead of the hotel last night. It was fun. I got to drink hot tea. We had to wait in line to use toilets and to get washed. Early tomorrow we will ride a bus to a place called Mount Arafat.

June 6, 1992

Dear Diary,

We stayed at Mount Arafat from morning till sunset. We took another bus down to a little hill. I saw Mom and Dad oicking up small stones. They said we will use them tomorrow.

How many kinds of car horns are there? I heard them all last night. Thousands of cars, trucks and buses were all making noise. We slept on hajj mats without any covers. The sky was clear and I saw millions of stars.

June 7, 1992

Dear Diary,

Mom and Dad said today is 'Id. It was not like back home. We walked and walked. We bought some Coke to drink, but it was not cold. We went to throw the small stones at Shaitan. I got scared there, too. We had to be careful where so many people were throwing stones.

June 8, 1992

Dear Diary,

I saw a lot of people crying while they read Qur'an and prayed. My mom cried, too. Reading Qur'an and praying in the Holy Mosque feels very special. Today I prayed extra special prayers for my family. I read the part of Qur'an called 'Amma during our trip. I like this trip, even though it is kind of hard. Dad says Allah gives us a big reward if we are patient.

June 9, 1992

Dear Diary,

Today Dad went to throw stones again. Mom and I shopped. People had things to sell spread out on blankets on the ground. At prayer time, the owners put up a curtain and went away to pray. They weren't afraid someone would steal.

June 10, 1992

Dear Diary,

Today we walked and walked. We climbed the mountain to Prophet Muhammad's cave. That's where the Angel Jibreel came to him. It was awesome to stand on the mountain and think about the angel talking to Muhammad. Tomorrow we are going to Medina. I'll pretend I am going on Hijra with Prophet Muhammad and Abu Bakr.

June 11, 1992

Dear Diary,

At the Prophet's Mosque in Medina, there is a special entrance for women. It was very crowded. Then we found a place to pray and sit down. It was very peaceful. It felt very special to see all the people reading Qur'an and praying there. Mom said that Prophet Muhammad's house used to be here. Tomorrow we will try to see the Prophet's tomb, where he is buried.

June 12, 1992

Dear Diary,

We prayed a special prayer for the Prophet and gave him our salaam when we stood at the tomb. Then we got a driver to take us to some other special places. We saw the mosque of two qiblah and the battlefield of Uhud. Medina is on flat land, not in the mountains like Mekka.

June 13, 1992

Dear Diary,

Tomorrow we will go back to the airport and fly home. This was an exciting trip. I hope I can come again sometime. I hope we have time to get presents for my friends in the airport shops. I'll help Mom spend all of her riyal money before we go.

Drawing by student, Luqman Abdullah

LESSON PLAN 4, STORY A: Young Muslims Worship Allah

TOPICS: Worship, Reciting Qur'an, Prayers, Learning, Family, History, Hajj.

PRE-READING ACTIVITY

1. Review with the children what the word "prophet" means [from Lessons #1 and #2]. Combine this lesson with Islamic studies to discuss how Prophet Muhammad (S) was a very special prophet who brought us Islam as Muslims know it today. Use age-appropriate materials to tell who Muhammad was and about his early life in particular, which is beyond the scope of these materials. Stories from the Sirah (Iqra' Publications), and stories from the Islamic Foundation are examples.

2. Define with the children the word "worship," suggesting that it means prayer, thanking Allah and asking Him for help, and doing other things that the Qur'an through Prophet Muhammad (S) taught Muslims to do. This lesson, together with Lesson #5, may be used in an Islamic studies unit introducing the Five Pillars of Islam.

LEVEL I (COMPREHENSION)/LEVEL II (EVALUATION AND ANALYSIS)

1. List the various ways children participated in Islamic worship named in the stories in story A (learning Qur'an, going on Hajj, reciting Qur'an [and in Lesson #5, story A, praying]).

2. Ask the children where they have seen Muslims worshipping in these ways (home, school, friends' homes, masjid). Have them tell what they have seen. (prayer, reading and learning to read Qur'an, celebrating 'Id, making Hajj with parents, etc

3. Show pictures of children and adults in different parts of the world learning Qur'an, praying, and going along on Hajj [see refs. Children of Allah, Atlas of the Muslim World Since 1500 and Islamic School brochures, Mosque scrapbooks, etc.]. Discuss some of the differences among the pictures as to the way the children are dressed, the kind of materials they use (slates or books, sheets of wood and charcoal, different types of mosques, etc.) Explain that all Muslims worship in the same way all over the world. They worship as Prophet Muhammad taught us through the Qur'an.

4. Finally, the teacher may broaden the concept of Islamic worship to include good deeds in general, such as sharing, helping, giving charity, teaching, etc. Discuss with the children how they serve Allah when they do good things. Have the children give their own ideas how they might participate in community worship of this kind.

5. This lesson may be combined with Islamic studies units on the Five Pillars, and with Lesson #5 in this unit, on how to pray.

LEVEL III (REINFORCEMENT, ENRICHMENT AND EVALUATION ACTIVITIES)

1. Make pendants with the words "Allah" and "Muhammad" in Arabic script. Start with lace paper doilies of any size. Make colored paper circles to the size of the center part. In pencil, write the word Allah or Muhammad in Arabic script. Have the child trace it carefully using white glue in a squeeze bottle, or the teacher may assist. Then, shake glitter over the word. Shake off excess. When dry, the pendant may be threaded with colored yarn or golden cord and hung as a necklace or wall hanging.

2. Have a Qur'an reading featuring the children, using suras the children are currently learning. You may want to have the children dress in special clothes.

3. Have an older child from the school [the younger the better] who is outstanding in Qur'an recitation come to the class to make a special recitation. Alternately, bring in an adult reciter from a local mosque.

4. Make a masjid dollhouse from a large carton. Cut large arches all around. Paint and decorate it, using a piece of carpet for the floor. Make clothespin Muslim dolls to go to prayer in it, using old-fashioned wooden clothespins from craft stores. Drape squares of white cloth with a hole in the center for clothes, tied at the waist with yarn. For women, fold square into a triangle and tie at neck. You may add yarn hair or turbans. Use a flattened ball of plasticine for a base. Have the children learn to say Adhan and bring all the dolls to the masjid.

LESSON PLAN 4, STORY B: Going on Hajj with My Family

TOPICS: Worship, Reciting Qur'an, Prayers, Learning, Family, Patience, History, Hajj.

PRE-READING ACTIVITY

1. Review the concept of obeying Allah, and mention that Hajj is an important kind of worship for Muslims. Mention that it is one of the five pillars of Islam; introduce or review them. Tell the children that every Muslim should try to go on the Hajj once in his or her life.

2. Remind the children of Ibrahim, and tell them that many of the things Muslims do on Hajj are to remind us of his important story. Explain to the children the story of the Hajj in simple terms, and why Muslims make Hajj.

3. Show the children where Mecca is, using a map or globe, and discuss how people might get there from different places. (ship, airplane, etc.)

4. Explain the term "diary," and tell how people sometimes write a diary of everyday things, or only for special things like going on a trip. The teacher may refer to a classroom journal which tells about daily activities. It may be useful to keep such a diary with the children for a few days before telling this story.

LEVEL I (COMPREHENSION)

1. How many days does the diary write about? (13 days) Which day is "Id? (June 7, the seventh day of the trip) Is 'Id at the beginning, middle or end of the trip? (in the middle)

2. What clothing did the family wear for Hajj? Describe the clothing for men and for women. (See Level III, Activity #3 below.)

3. Make a list with the class of all the places the family visited and the activities that went with it. Identify the activities with photographs from magazine articles like the ones listed below in.

4. What things did the diary mention which were difficult? (heat, thirst, being tired, crowds of people, etc.) What things were different from home? (sleeping in a tent, drinking warm soda, sleeping under the sky, shopping in the market, praying on the sidewalk, etc.) Discuss with the children how hard the trip used to be long ago (on foot or by animals, took over a year) compared with now. (by airplane, with hotels, cars, buses)

5. What did the diary mention that was especially nice on the trip? (reading Qur'an in the Holy Mosque, seeing the Prophet's tomb and mosque where he lived, seeing the cave of Hira, etc.)

LEVEL II (EVALUATION AND ANALYSIS)

1. Talk about the feeling of obedience and unity with other Muslims on the Hajj, using photos of the masses of Muslims who come together at the same time and same place, wearing the same simple clothes.

2. Discuss the difficulties of taking a trip. Ask the children what makes any trip both fun and difficult, using their experiences of long and short trips with their families. Remind the students of the line in the June 8th entry about helping the family enjoy a trip by being patient and not fussing, complaining and asking for too many things. Give examples.

3. Discuss the purpose of the Hajj to ask Allah to forgive our mistakes. Compare the ease of saying prayers every day and asking forgiveness with the big journey of Hajj to do that.

4. Tell the students that families are supposed to try not to argue at all during their Hajj journey, and to be very good, and not to kill any animal large or small while they are near Mekka. Discuss with the students the reasons for these prohibitions.

LEVEL III (REINFORCEMENT, ENRICHMENT AND EVALUATION ACTIVITIES)

1. Bring magazine pictures of the Hajj ceremonies (Aramco World Magazine, "Journey of a Lifetime," July/August 1992) to show the children what takes place on Hajj.

2. Have a parent or other guest come to the class to tell about their Hajj trip.

3. Dress dolls in the clothing used for Hajj and display them in the classroom.

4. Write a song or poem with the children about the activities of the Hajj.

5. Make a classroom model of the Kaaba, using cardboard cartons. Display posters with photos of the Kaaba and the Prophet's Mosque in Medina. These can usually be obtained at Halal Meat stores or can be received by mail for free from the Office of the Cultural Attache, Royal Embassy of Saudi Arabia, Washington, D.C. For your classroom display, you may also borrow items showing Mekka and Medina from parents of the children.

The New Prayer Leader

A boy named 'Amr bin Salama had a very important job. He told this story:

I lived at a place where the camel caravans used to pass by. We heard people talking about a man from Makkah, named Muhammad ﷺ. We heard that he was sent by Allah. We heard the people reciting strange words. They called themselves Muslims. The people said Allah spoke these words to Muhammad ﷺ. These words were from the Qur'an. I used to memorize those words whenever I heard them. The words stuck in my mind.

The people in my tribe didn't believe that Muhammad ﷺ was sent by Allah. They waited to see how strong he was. They waited to see if he would win over his tribe first. But I believed.

Then, one day news came. Muhammad ﷺ and the Muslims won many battles. They won the city of Makkah.

Now people wanted to join Muhammad ﷺ. They wanted to be Muslim. My father went to visit Muhammad and the Muslims. He went to learn how to be Muslim.

When he came back, he said, "By Allah, I have come from the Prophet, for sure!" He told us when to pray the five prayers. He told us how to pray. Then he told us to find the person who knows the most Qur'an by heart. He should stand in front of everyone and lead the prayer. He would be the Imam.

No one in the tribe knew more Qur'an than me! So they made me their Imam. I was only six or seven years old! I used to wear a short shirt like the other little boys. It had gotten too small to cover me enough. So the people bought some cloth. They made me a new shirt for my new job. I was never so happy with anything as that shirt.

From Hadith Sahih Al-Bukhari, 5:595

The Reader

Usama lives in a small village. He goes to the village school. In the morning, he waves to his mother and father. He waves to his small brother and sister. They are riding on a donkey cart. They are going to work in the fields. Usama is going to school with his friends. He likes school. He learns to read books there. He learns Qur'an, too.

After school, he plays with his friends for a little while. Then he goes to join his family in the fields. He helps his father and mother with the work.

In the evening, the family rides home on the cart. It is piled high with green food for the animals. They have cows and goats in the shed at home. Usama helps his mother and father feed the animals.

Usama, his brothers and sisters eat supper. Grandmother is there, too. She asks Usama, "Did you study for school tomorrow?"

Usama says, "I will get the lamp and study now."

After a while, Usama's father calls him. "Did you finish studying?"

"Yes, Papa," answers Usama.

"Will you read something for us?" asks his father.

Sure, Papa, what is it?" Usama is proud to read for his family. They don't know how to read, but they work hard so Usama can go to school every day. They are proud of him, too.

Papa has a letter from Usama's uncle. Their uncle lives in America. Usama reads the letter to his mother, father and grandmother. He tells them everything in it. "Tomorrow, in sha' Allah, we will get paper and pen. Usama will write a letter to Uncle Khalid."

"It is getting late now. Let us pray 'Isha and then you can read from the Qur'an for us, Usama," says Papa.

Usama stands between his father and mother and grandmother to pray. The small children sleep nearby. Then Usama takes the Qur'an from the shelf and unwraps it. He reads for his family as he learned in school.

They are very pleased with him. They say, "Al-hamdu lillah! He is such a good reader. He is such a good boy. Alhamdulillah!"

LESSON PLAN 5, STORY A: The New Prayer Leader

TOPICS: Belief in Allah, Family, History, Prayers, Worship, Reciting Qur'an, Learning, Respect for Elders, Serving Others.

PRE-READING ACTIVITY

1. "Provide some background on the life of desert nomads living with their animals; explain what a "camel caravan" is, and how they travelled from town to town, like Mekka and Medina, where Prophet Muhammad (S) lived. You may wish to show the children photographs of the desert, particularly of the Arabian desert from large photo editions (Aramco and Its World, Eternal Saudi Arabia, Children of Allah, etc.)

2. Briefly explain how people in those tribes, who lived far apart, gradually heard about Islam. Explain that some were slow to believe, while others believed as soon as they heard. Tell the children how Prophet Muhammad (S) helped to spread Islam with Allah's help to many people while he was alive.

3. Explain that this is the story of one boy in one of those tribes.

LEVEL I (COMPREHENSION)

1. Tell the children that 'Amr was very young when he first heard of Islam. Ask them how he learned the Qur'an from the travelling Muslims. (He heard them recite and memorized it easily.) Suggest to the children that perhaps he saw them praying, or reading Qur'an around the campfire at night.

2. Was 'Amr's tribe Muslim? (no) Remind them that the tribe wanted to see if Muhammad (S) would win. When he won, they wanted to join the Muslims to be like everyone else. [The teacher may extend this "bandwagon" concept with examples if he/she feels the children are likely to be responsive.]

3. Who went to visit the Muslims and learn about Islam? ('Amr's father)

4. What did he tell the tribe when he came back? (He told them how to pray and when to pray.)

5. Who should be the prayer leader? [Explain "Imam" if necessary.] (the one who knew the most Qur'an) Whom did the tribe chose? ('Amr, even though the tribe was a small boy)

6. Why did they make him a new shirt? (because his old one was too short for him)

LEVEL II (ANALYSIS AND VALUE BUILDING)

1. Discuss why it was so easy for 'Amr to memorize what he heard, why the words "stuck in his mind." (Allah gave him belief before his family and tribe and made it easy.)

2. Ask the children how 'Amr must have felt when he was chosen to be the prayer leader. Why was he so pleased with the shirt that they made for their young, new Imam? Discuss what makes the children feel especially grown up. (doing things independently, helping parents and younger children in the family, etc.) How did 'Amr's parents feel (proud of him), and how do the children think their parents feel when they do something very grown-up?

3. Discuss the five times for prayer, reviewing or using Lessons #2B and #5A, above. You may wish at this time to discuss the concept of schedules mentioned in the last vignette of Lesson Plan #2B, Level III, Activity #4, instead of using that lesson's story to launch the activity. Use the worksheet for that lesson as well as activities for observing the sun's position.

4. See I, #3 above.

5. Discuss 'Amr's shirt, and talk about how our clothes should be clean and neat when we pray. Discuss different types of clothing worn by men and women for prayer.

LEVEL III (REINFORCEMENT, ENRICHMENT AND EVALUATION ACTIVITIES)

1. See II, #10, above, and worksheet for sun's position at prayer times. [See Worksheet #1 from Lesson #2 on prayer times.]

2. On two layers of tagboard or brown paper, draw the outline of a long, simple shirt of the type worn at that time. Have the children cut it out and decorate it. Tape the two layers together. Punch holes at intervals about 1/2" from the edge, leaving neck and hem of shirt free. With yarn or string and a plastic needle (or stiffen one end of the yarn with tape or glue), have the children "sew" or lace the yarn through the holes to make a shirt. [EXTRA HINT: a very colorful project to make prayer rugs can be done in a similar way, with paper weaving, using construction paper cutouts for decoration, and putting holes in each end for knotting on yarn fringe. The children may enjoy making such rugs for their first experience of praying together at school.]

LESSON PLAN 5, STORY B: The Reader

TOPICS: Family, Parents, Helping at Home, Learning, Reciting Qur'an, Respect for Elders, Politeness, Kindness, Serving Others, Village/City (Rural/Urban Communities), Worship, Prayers.

PRE-READING ACTIVITY

1. To set the scene for the story, explain that people live in different kinds of places. Contrast "village" with "city" in terms of appearance and activity. If the children are very interested in this idea, you may read Busy Day, Busy People, (Tibor Gergeley, Random House) or similar books about town and city, or about life in a village. Ask whether the children in the class live in a city or a village. Ask whether they have ever visited a village/city (depending on reply). Elicit their descriptions with emphasis on differences they can describe.

2. Set the scene for the story, explaining that it is about a child much like themselves, who lives in a place very different from where you may live! Ask them to notice what is alike and different about Usama's daily life.

LEVEL I (COMPREHENSION)

1. Ask where Usama and his family live. (in a village) How do they get to work? (donkey cart) What kind of work do they do? (farming)

2. Where does Usama go every morning? (school) Why does he go there? (to learn reading, Qur'an and other things, just like the children in this class.) Where does he go after school? (He helps in the fields.)

3. What does Usama know how to do that his mother and father do not? (read) Why didn't they know how to read? (They worked hard as farmers and had no chance to go to school.) Did they want Usama to learn to read? (Yes, they worked hard so he could go to school.)

4. How does Usama help his family by reading and writing? (Qur'an, letters from their uncle in America) What other things might he help them with in reading and writing? [Take children 's suggestions.]

LEVEL II (EVALUATION AND ANALYSIS)

1. Ask if the family seems to be rich or poor — ask why they chose their answer. The children's observations and definitions may launch an interesting discussion.

2. List all the different ways in which Usama helps his family in the story. Have the children list all the ways in which they help their family at home with the work.

3. Discuss how Usama's parents feel about their son, the reader. What makes parents feel proud? Have the children tell about a time when their parents or someone else felt proud of something they did.

4. Talk about how important reading and writing are in our lives. What does reading and writing help us to do? (know how to do things from reading instructions, traffic signs, letters to people faraway, reading labels on food [See Lesson #6, Story B], learning and having fun with books, etc.) The teacher may mention that Allah says in the Qur'an that Muslims should learn to read , and that Allah taught humans about writing (Surat Al- 'Alaq, v. 1-5). Muslims should try to learn as much as they can and study hard.

LEVEL III (REINFORCEMENT, ENRICHMENT AND EVALUATION ACTIVITIES)

1. Ask how many of the children have relatives in another country or another city or state. Help the children to prepare letters (dictated or written) and/or draw pictures to send to a relative who lives elsewhere. Ask the parents' cooperation to address and stamp them, and let the class take them to a mailbox. This may be done as part of a unit on "Community Helpers."

2. See lesson Plan #8 A, Level III, Activity #2, Helper Certificates for jobs promised at home, which may be repeated more than once throughout the year.

3. Send home a tagboard sentence strip with the beginning: "I was proud of my son/daughter NAME when he/she ....." and let the parent fill it in. The children may draw a picture to illustrate the idea, then post them together on the bulletin board.

4. See Activities on classroom Qur'an readings, Lesson Plan #4, Level III, Activities #2 and #3.

A Boy Serves Prophet Muhammad ﷺ

Prophet Muhammad ﷺ was always very busy. He used to answer many questions. He helped people in trouble. Sometimes he had to travel.

He needed someone to help with visitors. He needed a helper when he travelled. He needed someone to serve him.

Anas was a young boy. His family brought him to stay with the Prophet. They said to Prophet Muhammad ﷺ, "Anas is a wise boy, so let him serve you."

Anas stayed with Prophet Muhammad ﷺ in his house. He helped him at home and on journeys.

Anas loved Prophet Muhammad ﷺ. He learned many things from him. He said that the Prophet was always kind to him. He never asked him about something he did. He never asked him about something he did not do. But Anas always tried his best.

When Anas was older, he told people how Prophet Muhammad ﷺ lived at home. He remembered many sayings of the Prophet. He helped people learn how to be good Muslims.

Hadith Sahih Al-Bukhari, 4:29; 4:143

Learn by Helping

Papa is making all kinds of noises in the garage. He's banging and pounding out there. We even hear a crash now and then. Some machines are buzzing and roaring. We just have to see what's going on.

When we call Papa from the door, he doesn't hear us. His head is bent over the big sawing machine. It makes a terrible, scary noise. Then it stops.

"Papa! What are you doing?"

"I'm making a swing set for the backyard, in sha' Allah."

"Can we help you? Can we work, too?"

"Yes, but you need to listen and do as I say. I don't want you to get hurt with the tools."

We help carry the long pieces of wood. Each of us takes one end. Papa takes the middle. My brother brings nails from the garage.

Papa wants to make a hole in the wood for the screws. I hold the measuring stick and count off inches.
"One...two...three.........................twelve." Then Papa gives me a pencil. He tells me to make an "X" where the hole will go. He tells me to put it right by the number "12." I make a mistake the

first time. I put the "X" by number 10. Papa says, "That's all right, we can measure again. We can erase it and make a new "X" in the right place."

"Al-hamdulillahi!" I get it right the next time. Papa brings his drill. It looks like a gun with a sharp needle on it. It makes a whirring, growling sound. I want to hold it. Papa says, "No, it could slip and hurt you." But he lets me push the button. He holds it. It makes a hole in the wood. We put big screws into the holes. We turn them a little, but it's too hard. Papa can do it. He has strong hands.

My brother watches Papa get a little saw. It looks very sharp. Papa's arm goes up and down. It goes through the wood, "KKHHH...KKHHH...KKHHH!" The wood is cut. My brother wants to try it. The saw gets stuck in the wood. "Slowly, and push a little," says Papa, "Try sawing this small stick."

He did it. I try it, too. Hey, it works! "Alhamdulillahi!"

In the backyard, we put the pieces together. Papa lets us hit the nail with the hammer. "Keep your fingers away!"

Our neighbors come to watch. They want to help, too. Papa says they can help, but he says, "Listen to directions and be careful!"

We show them how to hold the nail and hit it. We show them how to use the screw driver. We show them how to hold the wood while Papa saws it. We help tie the ropes.

Soon the swing set is finished. Papa says, "We have to clean up first. We have to put the tools away. We can't leave the extra wood here. It's too dangerous."

We all help to carry and clean up. Before Papa goes inside, he called everybody and said, "Thanks for helping. Remember, young people should never use these tools by themselves. You could be hurt very badly. Do you understand?"

"Yes, thanks for letting us help." Then we ride and climb on the new swings. "We made it ourselves! Alhamdulillahi!" It's fun to help and learn.

LESSON PLAN 6, STORY A: A Boy Serves Prophet Muhammad

TOPICS: Serving Others, Learning, Family, Helping at Home, Politeness, Kindness, Guests, Respect for Elders, Sharing, Manners, Obeying, Community Helpers.

This lesson could be used in a unit on "Community Helpers" or in a unit on "The Family." Its themes are serving and helping each other, and learning through helping and cooperating.

PRE-READING ACTIVITY

1. Define the word "serve," and "servant" [not in the story], explaining that these are people who help with everyday work like cooking, cleaning, carrying things and helping with children and guests in the house. You might also discuss the broader meaning of the word "serve," as in serving Allah and serving others. Explain that Allah put us on earth to serve Him by doing what He wants and by helping to serve our fellow creatures.

2. Present some context for the children to understand how people sometimes have servants in their homes to help, and why Anas' family wanted him to live with Prophet Muhammad (S).

LEVEL I (COMPREHENSION)

1. Why was Prophet Muhammad very busy? What did he do?

2. What kind of helper did he need?

3. What made Anas a good servant for the Prophet? (He was wise.)

4. How did Anas help the Prophet?

5. How did Prophet Muhammad (S) act toward Anas? Discuss what Anas specifically said about this (never asking him about doing or not doing something).

6. Discuss the kind of things Anas might have learned from the Prophet (rules about how to live, how to treat others, being patient in difficult times).

7. What did Anas do when he was older? How did he teach others what he learned from Prophet Muhammad (S)?

LEVEL II (ANALYSIS AND VALUE BUILDING)

1. Explain that Prophet Muhammad (S) was not lazy. He loved to do his own work, like cleaning his house, mending his clothes and shoes, and preparing food, and he always helped his wives. But since he had so many things to do, he needed help. He needed someone to serve him. Talk about how Prophet Muhammad (S) taught us to treat the people who serve us: he was always kind and polite; he always helped them with the work; he never gave them work that was too hard. Ask how many of the children may have people other than members of the family who help with work, such as housekeepers and babysitters. Ask the children for ways they can follow Prophet Muhammad's (S) example in treating them kindly (always speaking kindly and politely [saying "please" and "thank you" or Islamic equivalents], being considerate by not making a mess, picking up their own things, etc.).

2. By questioning the children and discussing their answers, bring out the ideas that Anas' family wanted to send him to live with the Prophet to help Muhammad, as a gift to him, and also to help Anas, since he could stay very near to Prophet Muhammad (S) and learn from him.

3. Build on the idea in I, #1 above by asking what a servant does, and that serving and helping are the same. Tell the children that Muslims are always supposed to help and serve family members and other people. The teacher may wish to expand on the idea of all people as servants of Allah, one meaning of the name Abdullah.

4. Discuss the idea of learning through watching, and also learning through serving and helping others. Elicit the children's experiences with something they have learned through watching parents or others. Talk about what we can learn by helping others, or what skills we learn in order to serve and help with household or other tasks. [These ideas will be expanded in Level II, Story B of this lesson, below.]

5. Explain to the children how Anas became famous as a companion who memorized many sayings of Prophet Muhammad (S) and told them to others. This was because he stayed close to him and paid attention. Show them some Hadith books where these sayings are kept. Explain that many Muslims all over the world know this companion's name and even name their children after him, even though he was a simple servant.

LESSON PLAN 6, STORY A: A Boy Serves Prophet Muhammad

TOPICS: Serving Others, Learning, Family, Helping at Home, Politeness, Kindness, Guests, Respect for Elders, Sharing, Manners, Obeying, Community Helpers.

LEVEL III (REINFORCEMENT, ENRICHMENT AND EVALUATION ACTIVITIES)

1. Make a picture chart of service tasks needed in the classroom, and rotate these tasks among the children. To mark whose turn it is, make "Helping Hands" in which each child traces around his hand on construction paper and cuts it out. Put the names on the hands with marker, and post them on the chart. A more permanent chart for the whole year can be made with cardboard hand tracings and the children's photos.

2. Have the children think of a service they can do to help a family member. Let them make a certificate for the person promising that they will do it. They may draw, dictate or write on the certificate, or the teacher may accompany the child's certificate with a note to the parents, including a place for the parent to sign, or a "Thank You" certificate to be filled out when the task is complete.

3. Teach the song about helping with household tasks "This Is the Way We Wash Our Clothes," adding verses and motions for sweeping, cooking, dusting, painting the house, fixing things (hammer and screwdriver), washing the car or anything else the children think of.

LESSON PLAN 6, STORY B: Learn by Helping

TOPICS: Serving Others, Learning, Parents and Family, Helping at Home, Politeness, Kindness, Respect for Elders, Sharing, Manners, Obeying, Community Helpers, Safety, Charity.

PRE-READING ACTIVITY

1. Ask the group if their parents like to do any special things like woodworking, baking, sewing, painting or other crafts and hobbies. Have the children tell how they can help with this kind of work. Ask what the family member has taught them to do in order to help. Explain that knowing how to do things is called a "skill."

LEVEL I (COMPREHENSION)

1. How did the children know what Papa was doing? (noise of tools)

2. What was he making? (a swing set) Have the children list items he used to make the swing set. (saw, hammer, measuring stick, drill, screws, hammer, nails, wood and ropes)

3. Did the children want to help? Did Papa let them help? Discuss what he said to them about helping. (listening and being careful with the tools)

4. Go through each activity the children helped with and talk about how Papa helped them to learn it (sawing, measuring, carrying drilling, screwing, hammering), and discuss the danger in using the tools mentioned

5. How did the children help their neighbors to learn what Papa taught them? Discuss teaching what we have learned to others.

6. What did they do before playing? (clean up) Why? (tools and wood scraps are dangerous.)

LEVEL II (ANALYSIS AND VALUE BUILDING)

1. Discuss some skill or activity that each child has learned by watching an older family member. (cooking, flying a kite, making something from wood or cloth, etc.) Talk about what some of the children teach their younger siblings. (getting dressed, building with toy blocks or bricks, making sandwiches, etc.)

2. Discuss some work or play at home that parents don't allow children to help with because it is too dangerous or difficult. Help the children draw an analogy to times when they don't want a younger sibling to "mess up" their own play because they are not skilled enough, or the game has small, dangerous pieces, etc.

3. Relate these ideas to the concepts in lessons #8 and #12 on respect for older people. We must show respect (listening, following directions, being polite) in order to learn what they know, and we must show our thanks when we learn from them. (love and kindness)

LEVEL III (REINFORCEMENT ACTIVITIES)

1. Have a parent, art teacher, or guest come into the classroom to teach the students a special craft activity. Discuss behavior and rules for learning something from a person who is skilled; why it is important to listen and follow directions, and to observe safety and other rules.

2. Help some students who may be willing to show the class members how to do something special they learned. (paper hat folding, making a house from "Lincoln Logs" or "Legos", etc.) Talk about following the rules as above.

3. Use Worksheet #2 to help with I, #2 above, as a comprehension exercise on the tools and materials used. Let the students draw lines from the tool to what it is used for.

Which Tools Do We Use?

Draw a line from the tool to the job it does.

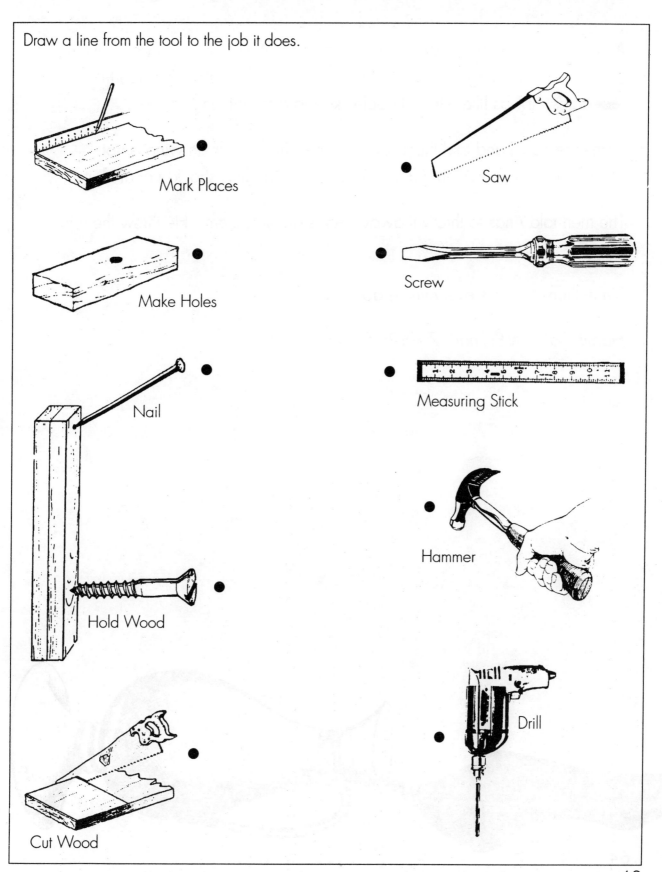

Mark Places

Saw

Make Holes

Screw

Nail

Measuring Stick

Hold Wood

Hammer

Cut Wood

Drill

Obeying Allah

Long ago in Prophet Muhammad's ﷺ time, Anas was serving his uncles. He was bringing them something to drink. It was a drink made from dates. It was like wine. People liked to drink it then.

Someone came and told them some news. They told them wine is not allowed any more. Allah made it forbidden. Muslims should not drink it.

The men told Anas to throw it away. Anas obeyed them. He threw the wine away.

Since then, Muslims everywhere do not drink wine.

Hadith Sahih Al-Bukhari, 7:489; 7:505; 7:526

What Muslims Shouldn't Eat

Kamal and his sister Maryam go to the store with their older brother Khalil. They are going to buy some candy. They are standing in front of a big shelf full of many different colors and kinds of candy. They will choose some candy.

Maryam sees a bag of candy. She says, "I want some of those!"

Kamal reaches for another bag. He says, "I like that candy! Let's get those!"

Their brother Khalil says, "Wait a minute. Mom says we have to read the bag first."

"But we can't read yet! Why do we have to read it?" say Kamal and Maryam.

"I can read it for you. We have to see what's in the candy," says Khalil.

"But why?"

"Sometimes things are in it that Muslims shouldn't eat. Like we can't eat things made from pigs. Allah forbids eating pigs. Allah wants us to

do what is good for us."

"But candy isn't from pigs," said Maryam.

Khalil read the bag. He said, "Uh-oh, Maryam, there's something in it that comes from pigs. We can't get these. You have to pick something else." He read the the bag tyhat Kamal had picked. "Sorry, Kamal, we can't eat these. Let's look for some other candy."

So they picked and read, and picked and read. Their big brother helped them get some candy that Muslims may eat. And it was very sweet, too.

LESSON PLAN 7, STORY A: Obeying Allah

TOPICS: Food and Nutrition, Halal and Haram, Obeying, Respect for Elders, Politeness.

It is very helpful if lesson #5 is done before this one, to identify Anas Ibn Malik and discuss his role. This story, together with Story B, may be used in a unit on Foods and Nutrition.

PRE-READING ACTIVITY

1. Review Anas' role as Muhammad's (S) servant from Lesson #5A.

2. Tell the children that this hadith tells the story of how wine was forbidden to Muslims during the Prophet's time. Explain what wine is and perhaps how it is made. Talk about similar alcoholic drinks which are all forbidden to Muslims.

LEVEL I (COMPREHENSION)

1. Ask whom Anas was serving, and what was the news that came to them. Explain that these drinks were not haram or forbidden at first, but this story is about the day when they became forbidden.

2. What did the men do when they heard the news? What did Anas do? Discuss how they did not finish what they had, and Anas did not wait or waste time, but they obeyed right away.

3. Explain what was the drink mentioned in the story, that it was like wine or beer or other alcoholic drinks [perhaps seen on TV by the children]. Tell the students that people used to make these drinks out of dates or grapes or other foods and leave them for a long time until they changed into wine. Talk about their effect on the body.

LEVEL II (EVALUATION AND ANALYSIS)

1. Build on #4, above, asking the children how fast we should obey Allah; how fast should we obey our parents and teachers when they ask us to do something. [Activity: The children may role play parent and child, making a request and fulfilling it, using the proper Islamic manners.]

2. Discuss with the children other things Muslims do in which they obey Allah. (believing, praying, helping others, being kind, etc.)

3. One of the most important concepts in this pair of stories is that Allah makes things forbidden because he wants our bodies and minds to stay healthy. He wants what is good for us, so we obey Him. Discuss with the children other things which are forbidden to do [see table of objectives in teachers' guide] because they are unhealthy.

LEVEL III (REINFORCEMENT, ENRICHMENT AND EVALUATION ACTIVITIES)
[See Activities for Story B, below.]

LESSON PLAN 7, STORY B: What Muslims Shouldn't Eat

TOPICS: Food and Nutrition, Halal and Haram, Obeying, Respect for Elders, Politeness.

PRE-READING ACTIVITY

1. Discuss with the group whether they have ever been told that they shouldn't eat certain foods. Make a list of the children's answers on the board or flip chart. Try to place the answers in categories, i.e., what they don't want them to eat because it is harmful to teeth or because of allergies, what is not good nutrition like "junk food," and certain foods not allowed to Muslims.

LEVEL I (COMPREHENSION)

1. Where did the children go? (to the store) What did they want to buy? (candy)

2. Who went with Kamal and Maryam? (their older brother Khalil)

3. What did Khalil do before they bought the candy? (He read the bag to see what ingredients are in the candy.) Explain the word ingredients.

4. What kind of ingredients did Khalil say they couldn't have? (things made from pigs) What kinds of candy might have ingredients from the pig in them? (candy or cookies with gelatin made from cooked animal bones)

LEVEL II (EVALUATION AND ANALYSIS)

1. See Level III, Activity #3, below, which is essential for comprehension of these ideas. Explain that while children may not read the ingredients, they should ask their parents or others to do so. More important, they should not make a fuss to have something when an adult or older child says Muslims shouldn't eat it.

2. Discuss why Khalil read the bag of candy or cookies first. Explain that their mother taught them to do that, so they can see what is in the food they buy. They didn't want to eat something haram by accident. Discuss what haram means [see Level III, Activity #1 below], and particularly that Allah forbid us things which are bad for the health of our bodies and our minds.

3. Ask the children whether Kamal and Maryam made a fuss with their older brother because they couldn't have what they first chose. Discuss the word obey and what it means to obey older brothers and sisters, parents, teachers, etc. Talk about how important it is to obey Allah, even though we don't see Him. He sees us always, and He wants what is good for us. Compare the behavior of the children in the story with the obedience of the children of Anas Ibn Malik and his uncles in Story A.

LEVEL III (REINFORCEMENT, ENRICHMENT AND EVALUATION ACTIVITIES)

1. Read and discuss selected pages from *My Little Book of Halal and Haram* to introduce some foods which Muslims may not eat.

2. Have the children color pictures of some animals Muslims are not allowed to eat from the book mentioned above.

3. Bring packages or pictures of candies and other food products popular with children which often contain haram ingredients, such as hot dogs, marshmallows, gummi-bears, gelatin, etc. Define the word "ingredient." and show the children an ingredient label. The most important concepts here are that (a) the children should ask if it is all right to eat and (b) haram ingredients are sometimes hidden in foods that look all right. Children should depend on adults and other older people to help them eat healthy, halal foods.

4. Building on these ideas, discuss other foods which are not haram, but which we should not eat too much of, such as sweets and "junk food." The Berenstain Bears, *Too Much Junk Food* is excellent for explaining this point. Discuss with the children that Muslims have a duty to take care of the healthy body which Allah gave them. General Mills Inc., Minneapolis, MN 55440, also has an offer to supply free Food Pyramid posters.

Aisha's Winged Horse

Aisha was a young girl when she met Prophet Muhammad ﷺ. She used to play with dolls and ride on swings just like children now.* Her father, Abu Bakr, was a very special friend to the Prophet.

*(See Hadith AL-Bukhari, 8:151[dolls]; 5:234[swing])

Once, the Prophet entered the house and found Aisha playing. A breeze came through the house and blew a curtain aside. Behind the curtain, the Prophet saw Aisha's toys. There were some dolls, and in the middle of them was a horse.

The Prophet asked her, "What are those, Aisha?"

"My dolls," she answered.

"What is that I see among them?" asked the Prophet.

"A horse," said Aisha.

Then he asked, "And what is that on it?"

"Two wings."

"A horse with wings?" asked the Prophet.

Aisha answered, "I heard that Solomon used to have a horse with wings."

The Prophet smiled broadly at the smart girl.

[Retold from the Hadiths related in Sayyid Sabiq, Fiqh Al-Sunna, vol. 3, p. 292-293; in Bukhari and Abu Dawud]

A Puppet Show: Our Toys

Characters (simple hand puppets):

Mother
Boy
Girl
Man

Props:

Miniature toys (cars, people figures, airplanes, etc.)
A small TV set, or small box decorated as a TV.
A puppet-sized cardboard box or carton
A cardboard car for the characters (see sketch)

Scene I: [The boy and girl are on stage, watching the TV]

BOY: Oh, wow! Look at that neat toy! It looks just like the monster in the cartoon! I want that!

GIRL: Yeah, but I don't think Mom will like that toy.

BOY: Why not?

GIRL: It's too ugly! She won't buy those yucky cartoon monsters. But she'll get me that doll! Look, it walks and talks and even eats and everything.

BOY: I don't know. Mom doesn't like some toys on TV. Let's ask her.

BOY AND GIRL: Mom!?

MOTHER: [comes on stage] Yes, my children?

BOY AND GIRL: Can we go to the Toy Store and pick out our 'Id presents today? Yesterday you said we could. Please?

MOTHER: Yes, we can go today. Our 'Id is coming soon. But first, let's do something for other Muslim children.

BOY: What, Mom?

GIRL: What can we do?

MOTHER: Let's go to the playroom and see.

Scene II: [Toy miniatures are scattered all across the stage]

MOTHER: What do you children see in here?

BOY AND GIRL: Toys, our toys.

MOTHER: Doesn't it look like a mess in here?

GIRL: Well, it's hard to keep everything picked up.

BOY: Yeah, there's no space on the shelves or in the toy box for all these toys.

MOTHER: That's what I think, too.

BOY: So what can we do?

MOTHER: Let's find some toys to give to other children for 'Id presents.

GIRL: But doesn't everybody go to the store to get new toys?

MOTHER: Some mothers and fathers don't have enough money for that.

BOY: Oh, I remember, last week we saw a big box for old toys at the Masjid.

GIRL: I saw that, too. My friends put some toys in there.

MOTHER: Let's hurry so we have time to go to the store. Go and get a big box.

[GIRL and BOY go off stage, then come back carrying a carton.]

GIRL AND BOY: **[Grunting and panting]** Here's the biggest one we could find.

MOTHER: Let's see, how about your old bike; it's too small for you.

GIRL: Ok. I have a big one, now. **[Puts it in the box]**

BOY: I don't need this train set anymore; it's for little kids, too. **[Puts it in the box]**

MOTHER: Let's find more nice things you don't use anymore.

GIRL AND BOY: **[Go around picking up things, putting some neatly in the corner, and some in the box, saying...]** We'll keep this, oh, we don't need that...etc.

MOTHER: Look, our box is full and the room is all neat now. Now we can go to the Toy Store!

BOY AND GIRL: We'll carry the box to the car.

[All exit]

Scene III: [Mother, boy and girl riding in their car]

Offstage sounds: Varooom, varoom, bbbrrrr, brrrrooommm.

MOTHER: Let's drive to the Masjid first and drop off this box.

BOY: Ok, but let's hurry to go to the Toy Store.

GIRL: There's the Masjid, now!

MOTHER: I'll park the car.

BOY AND GIRL: We'll carry the box.

[They get out of the car; a man comes on stage at the side opposite the car.]

MOTHER, BOY and GIRL: As-Salamu 'Alaikum!

MAN: Wa 'Alaikum As-Salam!

BOY and GIRL: We brought these toys for children's 'Id presents. We don't need them anymore.

MAN: We'll take them to the children who need them. They'll be happy to have 'Id presents. Jazakum Allahu Khairan! 'Id Mubarak!

MOTHER: 'Id Mubarak! Let's go to the store and get your 'Id presents!

BOY AND GIRL: Yay!! Let's go!

LESSON PLAN 8, STORY A: Aisha's Winged Horse

TOPICS: History, Toys, Halal and Haram (dolls and animal figures for children), Respect for Elders, Safety (toys).

PRE-READING ACTIVITY

1. Explain who Aisha was and her importance to Muslims.

2. Discuss the simple way in which Muslims lived long ago in the time of Prophet Muhammad (S). Describe the kind of toys children had in those days, and what they were made of (wood, cloth and clay). You might use a book from the library on archaeological finds or the history of toys to show some toys from long ago.

LEVEL I (COMPREHENSION)

1. Compare and contrast the toys mentioned in the story with those to which the children in the class are accustomed. (dolls, swings, toy animals) It might be fun to ask whether they would have had toy cars, bicycles, etc. Discuss with the children how toys look like things people use. Today we travel with cars and bikes. How did people travel then? (They used animals like donkeys, horses, camels, and even elephants)

2. How did Prophet Muhammad (S) find out what toys Aisha had? (The wind blew aside the curtain). What toys did he see? (dolls and a toy horse)

3. Why did Aisha say that the horse had wings? (because Soloman had a horse with wings) Explain who Prophet Soloman was.

4. Was Prophet Muhammad (S) pleased that Aisha had those toys? How do we know that he was pleased? (He smiled.) What would he do if he did not want her to play with dolls or animal figures?

LEVEL II (EVALUATION AND ANALYSIS)

1. Discuss how Prophet Muhammad (S) loved children [see love at Home, Islamic Foundation, Stories of Sirah, Iqra Publications], and how he took time from his busy schedule to play with children.

2. The issue may arise from some children whose parents do not wish them to have stuffed animals or dolls in accordance with the Islamic injunction against representing people and animals. This hadith is brought to bear in opinions by jurists that such things are allowed for young children. It may be necessary to deal with a variety of opinion and practice among Muslim families on this issue.

3. Discuss the types of toys that our parents often don't want us to play with [see Story B for expansion of these ideas] and why. (dangerous, ugly, expensive or useless, or showing things Muslims don't do) Explain that when our parents don't want us to have a certain toy, we may politely ask why, but should not fuss. Parents and teachers, on the other hand, should do their best to explain why they disapprove of certain toys to enable children to make sound choices of their own in the future.

LEVEL III (REINFORCEMENT, ENRICHMENT AND EVALUATION ACTIVITIES)

1. Read Stories from the Qur'an: The Hoopoe of King Soloman (Ahmed Baghat, Shorouk International).

2. Have the children color the page from Color and Learn the Names of the Prophets (Hamza, Kazi Publications)

3. Do Worksheet #3, "Toys Today and long Ago," helping the children to use visual discrimination to analyse the toys pictured. Encourage the children to color the toys from long ago in detail to focus their attention on the way they were made, their simplicity. The modern toys are merely circled. Use the worksheet as a bridge activity to the following two activities, or conclude with the worksheet.

4. Make a model of Aisha's horse from clay. Attach cardboard or clay wings. Explain that toys today are often made with machines, whereas long ago they were made by hand. Sometimes very simple things were used. Explain that we can still make interesting toys by hand. Make simple dolls from clay, straw or cloth as children had long ago. One method for making a cloth doll is by placing a ball of stuffing in the center of a handkerchief, tying off the neck with a piece of string, and making four knots in the sides and corners of the handkerchief for arms and legs. Features can be added with markers, paints or embroidery. Another interesting toy is a bird, made from a pine cone, using feathers or leaves for wings and tail, which are glued on or stuck on with balls of plasticine. A string is then tied around the center of the body. The

LESSON PLAN 8, STORY A: Aisha's Winged Horse

TOPICS: History, Toys, Halal and Haram (dolls and animal figures for children), Respect for Elders, Safety (toys).

other end of the string is tied to a short stick. When twirled around the child's head, the bird "flies."

5. Visit a toy museum. An important objective of this lesson is to cultivate a sense of history and change with time. Discuss with them the way toys were made, by machine and by hand, and how these toys look different from those we have today. Discuss similarities with the children's toys as well.

Toys Now and Long Ago

Circle the toys children play with today.

Color the toys children played with long ago

Teddy Bear

Cart and Oxen

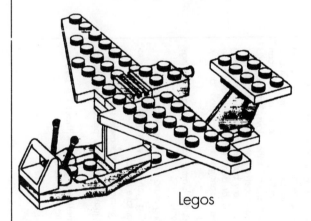

Legos

Straw Horse

Ragdoll

Car

LESSON PLAN 8 STORY B: A Puppet Show: Our Toys

TOPICS: Toys, Family and Parents, Respect for Elders, Charity, Sharing, Gifts and Giving, Politeness, Safety (toys), Environment (recycling), Money and Trade.

See Project Instructions for tips on how to stage this simple puppet show.

LEVEL I (COMPREHENSION)

1. Where did the children see the toys they wanted? (on TV) What did the boy want? (cartoon monster) What did the girl want? (doll)

2. Did their mother always buy what they wanted? (No, she didn't like some toys they saw on TV.)

3. What presents was the family going to get at the toy store? ('Id presents)

4. What did their mother want them to do before they went to the store? (She wanted them to clean up the toy room and choose some old toys to give away.)

5. What toys did they choose to give away? (toys that were too small or not used anymore) What did they do with the other toys? (They put them away neatly.)

6. Where did they take the toys? (to a box in the masjid)

LEVEL II (EVALUATION AND ANALYSIS)

1. Discuss why some parents cannot buy new toys for their children. Explain what families have to buy first when they have some, but not a lot of money, such as food, housing and clothes, gas for the car to get to work and similar necessities. Discuss the concept of things we have to have and extra things. Introducing the concept of wasting and using wisely, ask the children what would happen if their parents bought toys but no food, etc.

2. Leading into the concept of wasting things and not wasting things, discuss the choices for disposing of things which are no longer needed. (a. leaving them at home until the house is full; b. throwing them in the trash; c. giving the ones which can still be used to others who can use them again.) Discuss these alternatives, what kinds of things can be used again (clothes, toys, furniture), and who can receive them (friends with younger children, new babies, needy families whom we know or don't know. [This discussion can be a springboard for lessons on recycling.]

3. Discuss the Islamic manners for giving things to people:

   —giving without being proud or boasting

   —giving generously and not wanting to keep or take it back

   —not giving broken or useless or dirty things

   —not making a needy person feel shy or poor

   —sometimes giving without the person knowing who we are

4. Discuss the TV commercials in Scene I and how the children want what they see. Ask the children to relate their experience with TV ads — whether ads make them want things, and whether parents (should) always get what children ask for.

5. See Story A, Level II, Activity #3 above. Discuss the types of toys that our parents often don't want us to play with and why (dangerous, ugly, expensive or useless, or showing things Muslims don't do). Ask for the children's experiences with their parents refusing to let them play with certain toys; explore the reasons they understand. Explain that when our parents don't want us to have a certain toy, it doesn't mean that they don't love us enough. There is usually a good reason for their choice, and they mean something good for us. We may politely ask why, but should not fuss and insist. [Parents and teachers, on the one hand, should do their best to explain why they disapprove of certain toys to enable children to make sound choices of their own in the future.]

6. If this story is used around the time of 'Id celebration, discuss why children get new clothes, shoes and sometimes receive presents if their families have enough money. Discuss the importance of remembering needy families during the time of 'Id and of being generous. Use this practice to remind the children of all the things their parents do for them, and the need to be kind and grateful to them in return.

LEVEL III (REINFORCEMENT, ENRICHMENT AND EVALUATION ACTIVITIES)

1. Have the children use the puppet show script to act out a dramatic play.

2. Have a toy donation drive in the classroom, in which a note is sent home to parents asking for at least one outgrown toy. Encourage the parents to involve the children in selecting the toy to be donated. Find worthy recipients through mosques or other organizations, especially in time for 'Id.

3. Have a toy swap in the classroom, similarly asking the parents to help select inexpensive toys to swap, to allow the children to practice letting go and receiving. If the class is using these lessons in a unit on money and trade, the children might have a toy sale with play money, in which they are priced instead of swapped, or in which real money is used to sell donated toys, with the proceeds going to charity. Thus all the various possibilities for re-using and recycling old toys to friends and charity are modelled in #2 and #3.

PROJECT INSTRUCTIONS: A Puppet Show: Our Toys

This simple puppet show can be staged with a minimum of extra effort. The show runs approximately 20 minutes. If the children are willing, they might stage the show themselves for another class, or an older class could stage it for the kindergarten. The simple props are described below.

STAGE:

If you use a puppet theater, it must be one with a ledge on which to place the props. A low, narrow table can also be used and covered with a sheet or tablecloth.

PUPPETS:

Use family puppets, which are often available as ethnic families. You will need a woman, a man, a boy and a girl. Two puppeteers are required.

In addition, it is helpful to add a character puppet as a "narrator" or "master of ceremonies." Any cartoon character, such as Donald Duck, Mickey Mouse or Bugs Bunny can be used, or any other favorite puppet. This puppet can ad-lib, greeting and setting the scene for the children, asking the comprehension questions after each scene, introducing each new scene and asking follow-up questions at the end. He also closes the show.

PROPS:

All of these props are simple enough to be assembled or made by the class as a project.

A small box may be covered with black or silver paper and given a TV screen and some buttons. Pipe cleaners can serve as an antenna.

Toy miniatures can be used to represent the children's toys, like the ones given at fast-food restaurants. If the toys mentioned in the script are not available in miniature, the script can be adapted to what you can find.

Plans for the car are found at the end of the project instructions. Alternatively, a photocopy enlargement of an automobile advertisement can be made, colored with markers, and mounted on stiff cardboard with a holding stick. It should be large enough that the mother and two children can stand behind it.

If desired, a cardboard flat can be made at one side of the stage to represent the masjid. This is optional.

PUPPET CAR

1. Cut out the two parts of the car.
2. Mount the two halves on stiff cardboard.
3. Color the car with markers, paint or crayons.
4. Use a staple gun to attach a holding stick from light half-round molding or dowel. If not available, fold a narrow strip of cardboard and tape it to reinforce. Attach with packing tape.

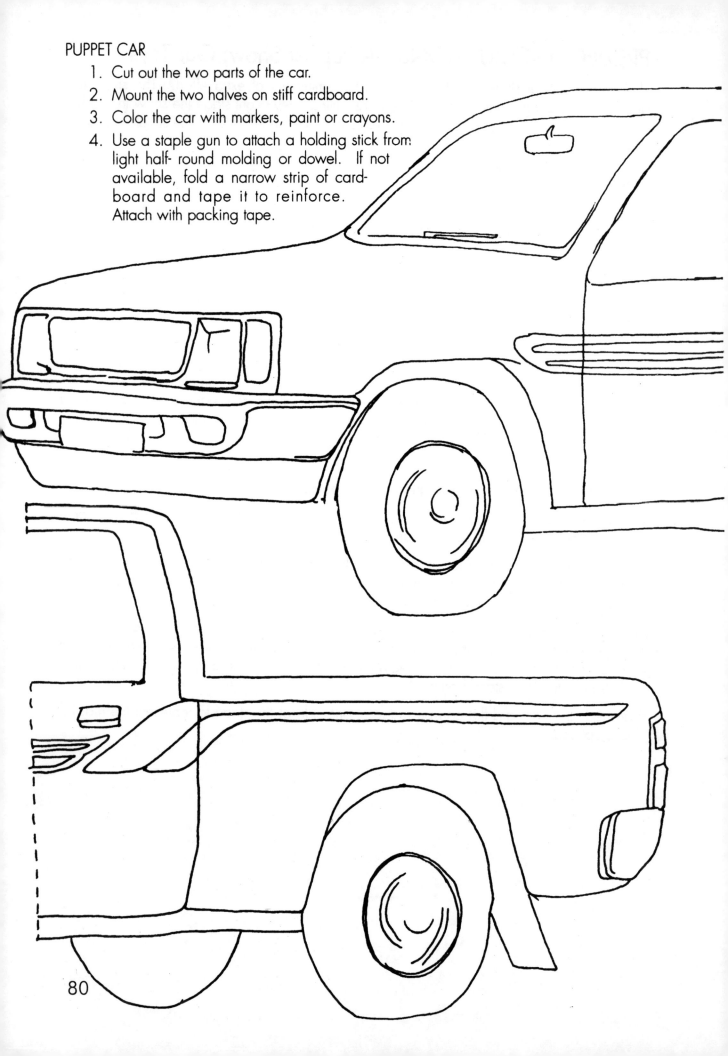

Sharing a Dish

A boy named 'Umar bin Abi Salama was staying in
Prophet Muhammad ﷺ. They used to share one di
'Umar told this story about eating with other people.

"My hand used to go around in the dish, taking food from the sides and the
middle. The Prophet saw me do that. Then he told me to say "Bismillah" and
eat with my right hand. He told me to eat only what is near to me in the dish.
He didn't want me to go around the dish looking for the best piece of food.
Ever since he told me that, I have followed his instructions when I eat."

From Hadith Sahih Al-Bukhari, 7:288:

Picnic

Some families went on a big picnic. Everyone brought some food to share. They put it on the picnic tables. The older people built fires to cook meat. They got the tables and the food ready to eat.

The children ran and played games together. They went down to the lake. They went up to the playground.

Then, the children heard a call, "Come to eat now!"

Everyone ran to the tables. The children were hungry.

Someone brought a big dish of chicken pieces. The boys and girls crowded around the dish. They started to grab.

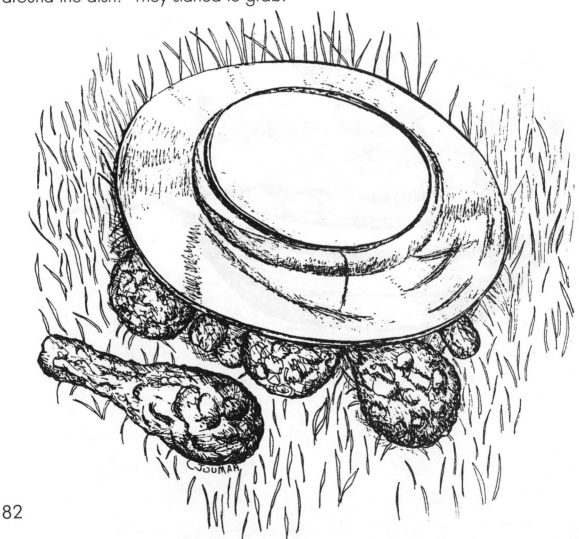

"Hey, don't push!"

"I want the chicken leg!"

"I want that big piece!"

One boy picked up a piece, then he put it down and took a different one.

Another boy said, "I don't want that one! You already touched it."

Some smaller children pushed their way to the dish. They wanted some, too.

"Hey, give my sister a piece."

"I need a wing for my little brother."

"WAIT, CHILDREN!" said one of the mothers.

Then it happened. With all the bumping and pushing and taking and talking, that dish fell right down on the ground. It fell upside down in the dirt and the grass. Now who could eat the chicken? It was all dirty!

Now the children were sad. They were mad. They started to argue more. "But you pushed me first!" "No, I was just trying to help my sister!" "You were grabbing!"

Two of the mothers helped pick up the chicken. They said, "We can wash off the grass and dirt. We can put it back on the fire. It will be all right."

While they waited, the mothers told everyone to sit down around the table. One said, "Is this the way Muslims share food together?"

"It's not a very good way," one girl said.

"Now no one can eat," said a little boy.

"Well," the mother said, "Prophet Muhammad ﷺ taught us a better way to share."

"First, wash your hands. Then, don't grab. Sit down and say ''Bismillah.'"

"With your right hand, take the piece nearest to you. Don't look for the biggest piece. Touch only the piece you're going to eat. That's how Muslims share their food."

Soon the chicken was ready again. This time, the children did a good job sharing. They shared potato chips and salad and drinks. And everyone had a very good meal.

And what did they say at the end?

"Al-hamdu lillah!"

LESSON PLAN 9, STORY A: Sharing a Dish of Food

TOPICS: Food and Nutrition, Cleanliness, Use of Right Hand, Manners, Politeness, Kindness, Sharing, Serving Others, Obeying, History.

PRE-READING ACTIVITY

1. Talk about how people ate in the time of Prophet Muhammad (S), sitting around large dishes of food and eating out of them with their hands. Explain that they didn't use plates for each person, or knife, fork and spoon like we do now. They ate with their washed right hand. They often used pieces of bread to wrap around pieces of food or dip into a soup. Many Muslim families still practice this way of eating, or use hands sometimes and utensils sometimes. Ask for a show of hands on this practice. Explain that when we do something as the Prophet did it, we say that it is Sunnah.

LEVEL I (COMPREHENSION)

1. Place a tray or dish of food cutouts from magazine, or play food from the classroom housekeeping center. Ask the students to demonstrate what Umar was doing with the dish of food as told in the story, or assist them by demonstrating.

2. Ask or assist them in demonstrating what Prophet Muhammad (S) told Umar to do when he shares a dish of food with others.

3. Write down and illustrate the steps for eating properly which are mentioned in this hadith.

LEVEL II (ANALYSIS AND VALUE BUILDING)

1. Taking the rules one by one from #3 (above), elicit the children's ideas about why Muslims are supposed to follow these rules in eating and sharing food, or conversely, why Umar was wrong in moving his hand around in the dish. The discussion may be best moved along by reading Story B at this point to illustrate.

LEVEL III (REINFORCEMENT AND EVALUATION ACTIVITIES)

Activities for both Stories A and B may be combined; see Story B Activities, below.

1. Prepare a meal for the class such as one mentioned in the Hadith collections: some bread, dates, cheese, milk and water. Have the students use flatbread as a spoon to dip into the food. The students could wear traditional Arab dress and sit on mats or rugs to add atmosphere. Before the meal, remind the students of the Sunna of washing before and after eating, of sharing the food on the plate, and using the right hand [see lesson #11] and rinsing the mouth after eating, and washing hands, as well as saying the dua' before and after eating.

LESSON PLAN 9, STORY B: A Picnic

TOPICS: Food and Nutrition, Cleanliness, Use of Right Hand, Manners, Politeness, Kindness, Sharing, Serving Others, Obeying.

PRE-READING ACTIVITY

1. Put some snack crackers or other treat on a tray and announce that you have something good for the children. See how they react. Do they take turns? Do they push and shove? When the confusion dies down, use this as an object lesson in how Muslims should learn to share food.

LEVEL I (COMPREHENSION)

1. Ask what happened to the plate of chicken at the picnic. Make a list of all the things the children did wrong, remembering Story A.

2. What did the children do after the food fell on the ground?

3. Get the children's ideas on why the food fell down.

4. What did the mothers do with the chicken to make it all right to eat?

5. What did the mothers tell the children to do when sharing the food? (Go over worksheet or list.)

LEVEL II (ANALYSIS AND VALUE BUILDING)

1. Talk about the feelings of the children and the parents before and after the food fell down.

2. Introduce the concept of manners and politeness and why we need them in dealing with people, using the events in the story. (They help people cooperate, they help people stay safe (not spreading germs and dirt), and keep people from being angry with each other, thus making us feel good about ourselves and others.)

LEVEL III (REINFORCEMENT ACTIVITIES)

1. Prepare a tray of treats of different kinds and colors and shapes. Remind the children what was said in the story, then the teacher may pass the tray, or the children may take turns being "host," passing it around the circle. The "guests" practice not delaying and not touching many pieces or hunting for a certain piece. It could be made into a game in which the group makes sure that no one touches more than the piece he takes by making the person who does so "OUT".

2. Make a poster for the classroom about the manners and rules for eating, using illustrations made by the children of the various steps in Muslim manners.

3. Combining with Islamic studies, learn some of the simple dua' used before and after eating. Practice them and the manners for eating in the lunchroom each day.

Sitting Next to Prophet Muhammad ﷺ

Prophet Muhammad ﷺ was sitting with some companions. Someone brought him a drink. He drank from the cup and wanted to share the rest with his friends. Muhammad ﷺ taught people that they should pass food or drink to the person on the right side. That day, a young boy was sitting on his right. On his left side, some old men were sitting.

The people loved Prophet Muhammad ﷺ. Everyone liked to take something from the Prophet's hand, or touch anything that he touched. They knew that it had a special blessing. This special blessing was that something good or healthy would come from drinking or eating after the Prophet of Allah.

Prophet Muhammad ﷺ knew that he should pass the cup to the boy on his right side first. But he asked the boy's permission to give the old men first. The boy answered, "By Allah, oh Rasul Allah! I will not give up my share from you to someone else!" So the Prophet put the cup in the boy's hand. The Prophet gave it to the boy on his right, even though he was very young.

From Hadith Sahih Al-Bukhari, 3.631; 3.774; 3.541; 7.524:

87

Doing the Right Thing

I have two legs and on them feet
For walking step by step.
I have two hands and when they meet,
You hear a clap-clap-clap.

My body has two separate sides,
A left one and a right.
They look alike, but they're not quite,
They're really opposite.

When we hold hands all in a line,
My right hand holding left on yours,
Your right side touching left on mine,
Like when we look in mirrors.

Allah made us with right and left,
To use in different ways.
He taught the Prophet what is best,
To live well all our days.

If you meet another Muslim,
Greet them first, for sure:
"Salamu 'alaikum, kaifa halkum"
Shake their right hand with yours.

When you eat, say "Bismillah"
Take food with your right hand,
Then say "Al-Hamdullilah!"
And pass to right-hand friend.

When getting dressed outside to go,
Do wear the right part first,
Right sleeve, right pantleg, or right shoe,
And follow with the left.

When taking off your clothes again,
Take left off first, hop to it,
Then take out right foot, leg or arm,
That's how the Muslims do it.

When you must go to the toilet,
Put your left foot through the door.
Wash with left hand, don't forget,
Step out with right once more.

When you are tired and it's night,
Lie down on your right side to sleep.
Say your du'a, turn out the light,
And pray Allah your soul to keep.

LESSON PLAN 10, STORY A: Sitting Next to Prophet Muhammad ﷺ

TOPICS: Food and Nutrition, Using the Right Hand, Passing to the Right, Sharing, Respect for Elders, Politeness, Manners, Serving Others,

PRE-READING ACTIVITY

1. Tell the group how people often brought food and drink to Prophet Muhammad (S), and how he always shared this and other presents with his companions.

2. Explain the idea of "blessing" or baraka as described in the children's lives. Give examples of blessings in the children's lives. (food, good clothes, health, family members, their houses, toys, etc.). Ask the children to name some more. [See Level III, Activity #2, below.] Explain how the companions used to compete for the Prophet's special blessings, like eating and drinking after him, or collecting the water from his wudu'.

LEVEL I (COMPREHENSION)

1. Ask the children which way Muslims pass things when they share. [Remind them of the story in Lesson #12 "The Picnic".] Tell them that Prophet Muhammad (S) taught us to take turns by passing things to the right-hand side.

2. Who was sitting with Prophet Muhammad (S) in the story? (a boy and some older men) Where were the men sitting? (to his left) Where was the boy sitting? (on his right)

3. What did Prophet Muhammad (S) ask the boy? (He asked his permission to pass the cup to the old men on his left.) What did the boy answer? (He politely said no.) Did he want to give up his turn to the old men? (No, because he loved to take his share from the Prophet.)

4. Did Prophet Muhammad (S) give the boy the cup first? (Yes)

LEVEL II (ANALYSIS AND VALUE BUILDING)

1. Ask the children why Prophet Muhammad (S) asked the boy to give up his turn. Take their ideas and opinions about whether or not the boy should have given up his turn.

2. Tell the children that Prophet Muhammad (S) was a teacher for all Muslims. Everything he did was a lesson. In this story, he was teaching:

   • how to take turns when sharing (passing to the right)

   • to be kind to older people

   • that everyone's rights and feelings are important

   • that both young and old people are important in Islam

   • that important people (even prophets and teachers) should ask permission before taking something important away from a person.

   It may be possible with some groups for the teacher to facilitate the children's development of some or all of the above ideas.

3. Discuss Muslims' love for Prophet Muhammad (S). Why did they love him? (Allah put love in their hearts when they believed; he was always kind and generous; he is the Muslims' teacher and leader, etc.) Read stories from Love Your God, Love at Home, and Love Your Brother, Love Your Neighbor(Islamic Foundation), and Stories of Sirah, vols. 3, et. al., to expand these ideas. Talk about what we do for people when we love them, and how the companions showed their love.

4. Discuss the idea of respect for older people [Refer also to Lesson #12, "Speaking Up"]. Ask why older people should be respected. (They take care of us, they know many things, sometimes very old people need our help and care.) Ask the children to name some ways in which we can show respect and kindness for older people (serving them first, talking kindly and politely to them, listening and obeying them, helping them).

5. Discuss serving guests at home, eliciting the children's experiences of helping to serve tea, coffee and other foods to their parents' guests. Ask whether older people are served first, especially grandparents and very old people.

LESSON PLAN 10, STORY A: Sitting Next to Prophet Muhammad ﷺ

TOPICS: Food and Nutrition, Using the Right Hand, Passing to the Right, Sharing, Respect for Elders, Politeness, Manners, Serving Others,

LEVEL III (REINFORCEMENT ACTIVITIES)

1. Role play serving guests at home, with a tray of drinks and cookies. Have the children serve the teacher(s) first, then around the circle to the right.

2. Invite the principal, office staff or school nurse to come to the classroom as guests whom the children can serve.

3. Roleplay talking to old people, using dress-up clothes, hats glasses and beards, with the children taking turns being "old" and "young," and practicing skills in talking with, serving and being kind to older people as discussed in II, #8, above.

4. Have the children name some of the blessings in their own lives as discussed in I, #1 above. Have them draw pictures of blessings we enjoy from Allah, like food, nice weather, toys, family members, friends, fun times, etc. Make a bulletin board or poster of these pictures, using an appropriate Qur'an verse as a heading.

LESSON PLAN 10, STORY B: Doing the Right Thing

TOPICS: Body Parts, Food and Nutrition, Using the Right Hand, Passing to the Right, Sharing, Respect for Elders, Politeness, Manners,

PRE-READING ACTIVITY

1. Have children identify their right hands and left hands, feet, sides, etc. Demonstrate how left touches right when we stand side by side or opposite one another. Introduce the poem by explaining that Allah taught Muslims to use their left and right sides for different uses.

LEVEL I (COMPREHENSION)

1. Discuss the fourth stanza, explaining that Muslims follow what Allah taught Prophet Muhammad to do in daily life. Allah loves us and wants the best for us.

2. Make a list of all the things Muslims should do with their right hand or right foot on a flip chart. List all of the things Muslims do with their left hand or left foot on the chart.

LEVEL II (ANALYSIS AND VALUE BUILDING)

1. Talk about right- or left-handedness in people, and how this is also from Allah, and not something to be sad about. It is just a difference between people, but that even left-handed people can follow the Sunnah in these listed acts.

2. Talk about why we should do various acts with left or right (speculation and conjecture) with the children. But explain that if we don't always know why, we do it because Muhammad (S) taught us, and he was guided by Allah.

LEVEL III (REINFORCEMENT ACTIVITIES)

1. Do several rhymes for learning left and right, like the old cheerleader chant, "Swing to the left, swing to the right, stand up sit down, right-right-right (while holding up right hand)." Another song is the sing-along, move-along, "Put your left foot out, put your left foot in; put your left foot out, and shake it all about….going through feet, knees, hips, shoulders, elbows, hands. This lesson and these activities are good accompaniments to a unit on parts of the body.

2. Decorate chart from II. #2 and post in the classroom.

3. Read the book Assalamu Alaikum (Islamic Foundation). Practice greeting and shaking hands with everyone in the group. Sing the greeting song "Assalamu Alaikum" from We Are Muslim Children (Saida Chaudry, American Trust Publications), which includes a cassette tape.

4. Practice putting on right shoes first, right sleeves, and taking off left sides first, perhaps using big shoes and coats for added dress-up fun. Children might do this as a relay race, with an aide as a helper.

5. Practice passing things to the right, using papers, objects and finally treats, which everyone eats with the right hand.

6. Teach the children to say the dua' for sleeping. If your class has a rest time, practice lying on the mats on the right side.

The Boy and the Dates

'Umar Ibn Al-Khattab was the second leader of the Muslims after Prophet Muhammad ﷺ died. He was a strong man and a very good fighter. He was wise and fair, and he liked to walk through the streets to make sure everything was in good order.

One day, some boys were playing in a grove of date palms. When they saw 'Umar coming, they all ran away, afraid that he might scold them. Only one boy named Sinan stayed. The lap of his shirt was full of dates. But he knew he didn't do anything wrong. He didn't throw stones at the dates high up in the tree.

When 'Umar came up to him, Sinan said, "Oh, Leader of the Muslims, I just collected the dates that the wind blew down!"

'Umar looked at him sternly and said, "Show me the dates so I can tell." He looked at the dates in his lap and said, "You are telling the truth!"

Then Sinan gathered up his courage and said to the great leader, "See those boys over there?"

"Yes," said 'Umar.

"If I go to them, they will attack me and take the dates."

93

So 'Umar walked over to them with the proud, brave boy at his side, and the boys did not dare to bother him.

From Ali and Naji Al-Tantawi, Akhbar 'Umar Wa Akhbar Abdullah Ibn Umar, p. 191.

At the Playground

Ali and Umar were on their way to the playground after school. "I'm thirsty," said Umar.

"I am, too. I have a soda in my bookbag," said Ali, "We can share it."

"I have some straws from school," said Umar.

"Bismillah," said Umar and Ali, drinking the soda, "That's good!"

There were many children at the playground in the park. Some older boys were drinking soda, too. Suddenly, Umar and Ali saw a soda bottle fly through the air from the direction of the boys. It broke on the cement. Big pieces of glass lay on the playground near the slide.

"Look, said Umar, "some children are up on the slide!"

"They're going to slide down into that glass!" shouted Ali.

"It's dangerous! They might get cut!"

Just then, a police car stopped by the playground. The police saw someone throw glass as they drove by.

The boys on the basketball court saw the police, too. They ran away into the street on the other side.

Umar and Ali have only one bottle. "What if the policeman thinks we did it?" Umar asked Ali. They start to run away.

"But what about the kids on the slide? We have to go tell them not to come down," said Ali.

So they didn't run away. Ali ran up the slide from the bottom to catch the younger kids. Ali told the kids not to slide down on the broken glass.

When the policeman came over, he looked at the boys. He saw the bottle in Umar's hand. He looked at the broken glass.

Ali said, "We didn't throw it. Some big boys threw it from the basketball court. They ran away."

"Where's your soda bottle?" the policeman asked Ali.

"My friend didn't have one," said Ali. "We shared mine with these straws. See?"

The policeman looked at the two boys and the straws sticking out of the bottle. He said, "You must be telling the truth. But why didn't you run away?"

"We saw the glass fall beside the slide. We saw the little kids sliding down. We didn't want them to get cut on the glass. We went up to tell them."

The policemen said, "You were very brave. Thank you for helping the children."

One officer said to the other one, "Let's get this glass cleaned up. Please bring a broom from the squad car."

The children found a bag and gave it to the policemen. They thanked the children and put broken glass into the bag. They let the two children wear their hats while they watched. The officers put the glass in the trash can. Before they drove away, the officers pinned silver badges on Ali's and Umar's shirts. Each one said "Police Helper" in blue letters.

Umar and Ali felt very proud. On their way home, they passed the boys who had run away. The silver badges shone in the sun. They hoped those big boys felt very ashamed.

LESSON PLAN 11 STORY A: The Boy and the Dates

TOPICS: Telling the Truth, Community Helpers, Assertiveness, Honesty, Respect for Elders, Serving Others, Stealing, History.

PRE-READING ACTIVITY

1. Explain who was 'Umar Ibn Al-Khattab. Some other anecdotes and stories about him may help to explain why people respected and feared his displeasure, and how he used to walk about among the people. [See Stories of Sirahllqra Foundation, The Kingdom of Justice and The Persecutor Comes Home (both Islamic Foundation).]

LEVEL I (COMPREHENSION)

1. What were the boys doing when 'Umar came along? (playing in a grove of date palms) Explain and/or show a picture of how dates grow, and how the trees are planted in a group called a grove.

2. What did the boys do when they saw 'Umar? (All ran away except Sina.)

3. How did Sina get the dates in the lap of his shirt? (He collected the ones that fell down from the wind.) How did 'Umar know that Sina got his dates from the ground and not from throwing stones at the tree. ('Umar could tell by looking at them.) Discuss how the dates might look if they fell by themselves — ripe and brown, the stem shrivelled and dry where it fell off. Compare with apples or other fruit the children may have seen.

4. Why did 'Umar walk with Sina to the boys? (to protect him from them)

LEVEL II (ANALYSIS AND VALUE BUILDING)

1. Discuss why Sina did not run away. (because he knew that he didn't do anything wrong [Later, compare this with the characters in Story B, who didn't run away because of the broken glass near the slide, wanting to help the other children.])

2. Ask how Sina probably felt when all the boys ran away except him. Discuss the "herd instinct" with the children as the idea that it is difficult sometimes to be different when everyone seems to be going one way. Give examples of various situations when children should follow the group, and when they should not.

3. Talk about telling the truth and not being afraid to do so, even when we do something wrong. Tell the old story about George Washington and the cherry tree, and explain how even when we do something wrong, our parents are not as angry if we tell the truth. Explain that sometimes, the truth can save someone's life, such as when we have accidentally put someone in danger with our play.

4. Explain that Prophet Muhammad (S) had the nickname "Al-Saddiq Al- Amin" because he always told the truth. Elicit the children's experiences with telling and not telling the truth. Discuss what can happen when we lie (the old proverb, "A lie has short legs"). 10. Talk about the relationship between saying the truth and being honest. Sina told 'Umar the truth, but he was honest in the first place, because he only took the dates that fell down. Give familiar examples of honest behavior [See lesson #2, "I Want It," on examples of not dealing honestly, such as stealing and not being fair to others.] Emphasize how important it is for Muslims to be both truthtellers and honest people.

LEVEL III (REINFORCEMENT, ENRICHMENT AND EVALUATION ACTIVITIES)

1. Tell the Aesop fable of "The Boy Who Cried Wolf" to illustrate that it is bad when people don't believe liars even when they do tell the truth. Make masks to act out the story.

2. Show the children library book pictures of the date palm and how it is grown in groves.

3. Make up a game building on the idea of following the group, something like "Follow the Leader," but make up situations when the group should and should not follow the leader, in order to practice discriminating. Use examples from Level II, Activity #2 above, such as throwing a piece of trash on the ground; crossing the street without looking or on red; pretending to hit another child; alternate these with active movements which the children do follow.

LESSON PLAN 11, STORY B: At the Playground

TOPICS: Telling the Truth, Community Helpers, Assertiveness, Honesty, Respect for Elders, Serving Others, Safety, Environment, Cleanliness, Kindness, Neighbors.

This pair of stories can be used in a unit on safety and community helpers, as well as personal social development.

PRE-READING ACTIVITY

1. Talk about playgrounds and safety. Discuss what belongs on a playground and what does not. (trash, sharp sticks, etc.) Elicit the children's experiences with finding trash or broken glass in a park or playground. Ask what the children should do if they ever found these things in play areas. (tell an adult, etc.) Introduce the story topic.

LEVEL I (COMPREHENSION)

1. Who was drinking soda at the playground? (Ali and Umar, and some older boys) Who threw the soda bottle? (an older boy)

2. What happened to the bottle? (It fell near the slide and broke.) Who saw the bottle break? (Ali and Umar, and the police in the squad car)

3. Who ran away from the police and who did not? (The big boys ran; Ali and Umar did not.)

4. Why didn't Ali and Umar run away? (They wanted to warn the children about the broken glass.) Were they afraid of the policemen? (They were afraid that the police would think Ali and Umar threw the glass.) How did they help the children? (They climbed up the slide and told them about the danger.)

5. How did the policeman know that Ali and Umar were telling the truth? (Because they had one bottle and two straws for sharing the soda.) The teacher may compare this with 'Umar Ibn Al-Khattab examining the dates in Sina's lap from Story A.

6. How did Ali and Umar help the police? (They helped them sweep up the glass.) What did the police give Umar and Ali? (They let them wear their police hats, then they thanked them and gave them silver badges.)

LEVEL II (ANALYSIS AND VALUE BUILDING)

1. Ask the children whether Ali and Umar felt afraid of the police. Talk about how it feels to know you are telling the truth, but sometimes adults don't believe you. Discuss why big people sometimes don't believe children. (forgetting, telling tall stories, using their imagination a lot) Talk about praticing telling the truth when it is important, and using imagination only for playing.

2. Discuss why the older boys felt afraid of the police, because they knew that they did something wrong. Elicit the children's experience of feeling that they did something wrong. Explain that Allah gave us uncomfortable feelings of shame and fear so that we can do good things instead of bad. Discuss the last line of the story, "They hoped those big boys were very ashamed."

3. Discuss Ali and Umar's feelings of concern for the children on the slide, and how wanting to help them made the boys very brave. Talk about bravery, and how doing good things can make us stronger than our fear. The teacher may review other stories in this unit (see topic index) or use other stories [See Level III, Activities #1 and #2, below] to expand on the concept of courage and bravery. Explain that just as Allah gave us uncomfortable feelings about doing bad things, He gives us strength and courage to do good things.

4. Talk about praying to Allah for strength when we are afraid, and teach special du'a to use when we are in difficulty.

5. Discuss what it means to be a good citizen in any country where you live. Make a list of things children can do to help keep their community safe and clean.

6. A final point to be raised in the story is the feeling of pride that comes from doing something courageous. Discuss Ali's and Umar's feeling when the police rewarded them, and when they saw the boys who had thrown the bottle and run away. Discuss the Muslim's need to thank Allah for the strength and courage He gave us and to be humble, not proud and boastful. Teach the Islamic expression La howla wa la quwwata illa bi Allah (There is no strength or force except with Allah).

LESSON PLAN 11, STORY B: At the Playground

TOPICS: Telling the Truth, Community Helpers, Assertiveness, Honesty, Respect for Elders, Serving Others, Safety, Environment, Cleanliness, Kindness, Neighbors.

LEVEL III (REINFORCEMENT, ENRICHMENT AND EVALUATION ACTIVITIES)

1. Read stories about bravery such as *Stories of Sirah* (Iqra Foundation), *The Courageous Children* (Islamic Foundation), *Aesop's Fables* and even selected episodes of superhero stories or comics. In discussing the stories, point up what made the characters able to overcome fear. Some of these stories may be used to point out the difference between courage and bravado, and pride and boasting.

2. Make a superhero cape and have the children act out scenes of rescue and good deeds of their own invention.

3. Make a poster with the children's pictures of practicing good citizenship.

4. Invite a community helper such as a fireman or a policeman to make a presentation on safety in the home and community. Explain or make a reverse presentation like a song or a play for the guest on what the students have been learning about Islam and good citizenship.

5. Discuss playground safety. Make a poster and/or a play which demonstrates the rules for safety on the playground.

The Prophet's Riddle

Ten of the companions were sitting with Prophet Muhammad ﷺ. He asked them a riddle, saying, "Tell me what tree is like a Muslim. Its leaves do not fall off, and it does not fall down. It gives fruit from time to time."

One of the companions was Abdullah, son of 'Umar. He thought he knew the answer. He wanted to call out, "It is the date palm tree, oh Allah's Prophet!" But he didn't speak. He looked around and saw that he was the youngest one sitting. All around him were older, important people. So he was shy and kept quiet.

When no one else answered, the Prophet said, "It is the date palm tree." ·

After they left that place, Abdullah told his father that he had known the answer to the riddle. "Why didn't you speak?" asked 'Umar. "I didn't see you or anyone speaking, so I didn't." His father told him he would have been very pleased if Abdullah had answered the Prophet's riddle.

Hadith Sahih Al-Bukhari, 6:220; 7:355

The Brothers and the Sticks

A father was sitting with his five sons. He wanted to see how strong and clever they were. He brought five sticks. He tied them together with a strong rope. Then he showed them to his sons. He said, "Who can break these five sticks?"

The oldest brother said, "I am very strong, I can do it! I have the strongest muscles." He took the sticks. He tried to break them with his hands. They didn't break.

The next oldest brother said, "I can do it. I am stronger." He tried with his hands, too. Nothing happened. He tried to break them over his knee. The sticks stayed the same.

The next brother tried to break them over the table. They didn't even crack.

The next brother leaned the sticks against a stone and jumped on them. He gave a big grunt and roar as he said, "I can do it, I'm super strong." The sticks flew up in the air and fell back down on the ground. The sticks were not broken.

The youngest brother was watching his big brothers. He saw that they couldn't break the sticks. He wanted to do it. His father would be proud of him. But all his brothers were bigger and older. If they couldn't do it, how could he?

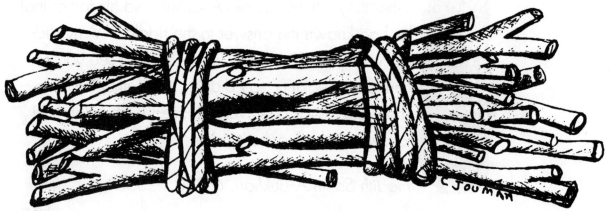

As he watched, he had an idea. "Why don't they take the rope off and break the sticks one by one?" he thought. "No, that can't be right. That's too easy." So he kept quiet.

Then their father said, "It's a hard job, my sons, isn't it?" Then he looked at his youngest son. He said, "Who can give it one more try?"

The littlest brother thought. "Will they laugh at me if I say it? Will they think that I'm not strong?" Then he thought, "It can't hurt to try! After all, they all tried."

"Well, boys?" said their father, "Do you give up?"

"Give me the sticks," said the youngest, "I'll try."

So he took the sticks. He untied the rope and took out the first stick. He snapped it in two. And the next, and the next, until all were broken on the ground. Then he smiled and said, "I did it. Is that right?"

"Right, my youngest son. You did some good thinking."

"But he took them apart!" said the others, "That's cheating!"

"I never said HOW you should break them," said Father. "But you all wanted to show how strong you are, and you forgot to think. I'm glad that the youngest of you was not afraid to try."

Then he told them all, "Remember, if you find something too difficult all at once, do it little by little."

LESSON PLAN 12, STORY A: The Prophet's Riddle

TOPICS: Assertiveness, Respect for Elders, Family, Parents, Learning, Manners, Politeness, Science & Math crossover.

PRE-READING ACTIVITY

1. Define the word "riddle" with the children, giving examples of riddles from a book or from memory. This story could become the anchor for a lesson about riddles. [See Level III, Activities #1 and #2, below.]

LEVEL I (COMPREHENSION)

1. Discuss first what happened when Prophet Muhammad (S) asked his companions to answer the riddle. (No one answered.)

2. Ask who knew the answer, but did not answer. Why did Ibn Umar not answer? (youngest one present, everyone else was quiet, perhaps afraid of being wrong)

3. Who did Ibn Umar tell that he knew the answer? Did his father wish Ibn Umar had spoken?

LEVEL II (EVALUATION AND ANALYSIS)

5. Discuss Ibn Umar's feelings of shyness which made him keep quiet. Several points may arise: his feeling that he was the youngest and not so important; being afraid to be different (to speak when others are silent); being afraid to give the wrong answer. The fact that he did not speak out because of respect for his elders is explored in the story "Respect for Elders" in *True Stories for Children* [TaHa Publishers], which discusses the same hadith, omitting "Umar's reply that he would have been pleased if his son had answered.

6. Discuss Ibn Umar and his father's feeling of pride/disappointment when they realized that he had the right answer.

7. Finally, discuss the content of the riddle as Prophet Muhammad described it:

   a. The date palm tree is like a Muslim

   b. Its leaves do not fall off

   c. It does not fall down

   d. It gives fruit

   The children will need some background on the importance of the date palm to people in Muhammad's time. Show them photographs of the tree, and tell the children how they sometimes had no other food than dates, and even the animals ate them. [Let the children eat some dates.] Talk about how tall and straight the tree was, and how it lived for a long time, and never lost its strong leaves, which were used to make mats, ropes, baskets, sandals, house roofing and many other things. [If possible, show them a basket or mat or leaves from the palm tree, or pictures of same.] Tell how the desert people depended upon its vitamin-rich, nutritious food each year, which they also sold for money and other goods. With this background, the class may draw conclusions about why Prophet Muhammad (S) compared a Muslim to this important tree. [See Activity #1 below to extend the description of a good Muslim to things familiar to the children.]

LESSON PLAN 12, STORY A: The Prophet's Riddle

TOPICS: Assertiveness, Respect for Elders, Family, Parents, Learning, Manners, Politeness, Science & Math crossover.

LEVEL III (REINFORCEMENT ACTIVITIES)

1. Use Worksheet #5 "A Date Palm Gives..." to add to the children's knowledge about this tree which is often mentioned in hadith literature. Have them color it carefully and discuss possible other uses. See activities with date palm, above in III, #3, and tasting dates, for which several varieties large and small, dried and fresh might be sampled.

2. Make up more riddles on the theme of "A Muslim is like a...." which illustrate the good qualities of a believer. The children may draw pictures of their ideas. This would make a nice wall display.

3. Read Shel Silverstein, *The Giving Tree* (Harper, 1964). Non-fiction books about useful plants and trees may be added to form a lesson on what Allah (ST) has provided for us.

4. Use this lesson as a bridge for other riddle activities involving math, science and literature. Math word problems, for example, could be phrased as riddles, or identification of plants or animals, etc. in science lessons. Books of riddles using word plays and jokes are good literature lessons which are readily available in libraries. One example is Rodney Peppe', *Hey Riddle Diddle* (Longman, 1971).

5. Play the game of "Concentration" using picture cards, in small or larger groups. Have the children raise their hand when they think they know where a "match" is. Start with a small number of cards and then increase the number to make it more challenging. Memory skills, raising hands to answer, and confidence are skills practiced in this activity.

A Date Palm Gives...

Roofs for Houses

Wood for Houses and Tools

Food for People and Animals

Rope

Baskets

Mats

LESSON PLAN 12, STORY B: The Brothers and the Sticks

TOPICS: Assertiveness, Respect for Elders, Family, Parents, Learning, Manners, Politeness, Problem-Solving.

This lesson may be used in a variety of cross-disciplinary activities involving problem-solving, riddles, science, math and literature (fairytales and fables).

PRE-READING ACTIVITY

1. Discuss the meaning of "fable," as a story which has a special moral or meaning. To provide examples, find out how many children in the group know the story of "The Lion and the Mouse," or "The Boy Who Cried Wolf." Tell one or both of these stories, ending preferably with the first, which is related to the meaning of the following story.

LEVEL I (COMPREHENSION)

1. How many sticks are in the story, and how many brothers?

2. What does the father want his sons to do? Did he say how to do it?

3. What did each brother try to do? Why did each brother say about himself?

4. Did the older brothers break the sticks? Why not?

5. What idea did the little brother have? What did he say about himself? Did he think he was strong and smart?

6. What did the little brother do with the sticks?

7. What did his father say when he broke the sticks?

LEVEL II (ANALYSIS AND VALUE BUILDING)

1. Discuss the way the older brothers approached the problem their father gave them. Ask the children what they said about themselves, and how they wanted to show off their strength.

2. Ask the children how the youngest brother felt about his idea to break the sticks one by one. Discuss his various feelings:

— being afraid to be different and try something new

— feeling that you're not as important as others

— knowing something but being afraid to be wrong

— a young person knowing something the older ones do not

Elicit the children's experiences of these feelings, having them share something which happened to them. Talk about the situation in a classroom, when a child feels shy about answering the teacher, and feelings about other children knowing more than oneself.

3. Both of these stories involve the topic of the behavior of young people toward older ones. Explain that it is good for young people to speak up, but they must do so politely, taking turns and not trying to drown out the voices of their elders.

4. With some children, it may be possible to engage in discussion about having the courage to be different, to speak up about something even when others do not. Someone in the group may be able to relate a firsthand experience.

LEVEL III (REINFORCEMENT ACTIVITIES)

1. Have the children try what is done in the story with a bundle of small sticks of various strengths. Draw out the analogy to yarn, thread, ropes and cables which are made up of many weak strands which combine for great strenth. Have the children test these materials by taking them apart to see how weak the individual fibers are.

2. Following Activity #1, above, discuss with the children the idea of cooperation, of weak individuals working together to do things they could not do alone. Read the Aesop's Fable "The Father and the Sticks" from which this story is adapted for that interpretation of the story. Here, the father shows that the sticks can be broken only when they are separated, so he tells his sons to stay together and find strength together. Read also the verse from the Qur'an, Sura III, verse 103: "And hold fast, all together, by the rope which God (stretches out for you), and be not divided among yourselves...," continuing to verse 105. Discuss cooperation and working together to please Allah and to succeed.

3. Model the proper behavior for asking permission to speak in a group, such as raising hands, waiting for one's turn, and saying "Excuse me." Call attention to this correct behavior during group discussion. Discuss and model through role play how young people may ask permission to speak when their parents or other older family members are talking together. Discuss the proper respect and manners, not interrupting, being patient while they finish, and polite ways to address older people. The children may enjoy wearing dress-up clothes to take turns role-playing this behavior.

LESSON PLAN 12, STORY B: The Brothers and the Sticks

TOPICS: Assertiveness, Respect for Elders, Family, Parents, Learning, Manners, Politeness, Problem-Solving.

4. This lesson can also be used as a springboard to problem- solving activities in math and science. Some of these might be found in brain teaser books, such as those from the Shari Lewis Playalong PBS TV show, which are age appropriate. Familiar ones include making figures out of toothpicks or cotton swabs. Other books on problem solving and critical thinking exercises for young children are increasingly available on the market.

Kindness to Animals

One of the companions of the Prophet, Ibn 'Umar, entered the house of his friend. He saw a young boy throwing a stone at a hen. The hen was tied up so it could not fly away. Ibn 'Umar untied the hen. He brought the boy and the hen and told his father, "Don't let your boys tie the birds and try to kill them.

I heard the Prophet say, 'Don't kill an animal or other living thing after tying it.'"

From Hadith Sahih Al-Bukhari 7:422

The Animals' Complaint

One summer day, some animals were in a meadow. A cow sat under a tree, chewing on some sweet grass. Some flies sat on her horns. A bird sat on her nest in the tree. Her chicks chirped noisily. A worm, a spider and a family of ants worked near the trunk of the tree. Some hens were pecking away at the ground in the shade around the tree.

On the other side of the meadow, some children were sitting on the fence. The bird saw them first.

"I hope those children aren't coming over here!" she whistled. "They always make trouble for us!"

The Cow cleared the grass out of her throat, "Moooo! I'll say! We give our milk to make the children strong, but they climb on the fence and throw clumps of mud at us. We just want to chew the grass and enjoy the sunshine."

The Hens clucked in, "We give up our eggs, just so they can fry them and scramble them and boil them. But do they thank us? No! The children like to run after us shouting and waving their arms. They scatter us all over the yard. I'm about to lose my feathers from fright!"

The insects started murmuring all together. "Talk about scaring

110

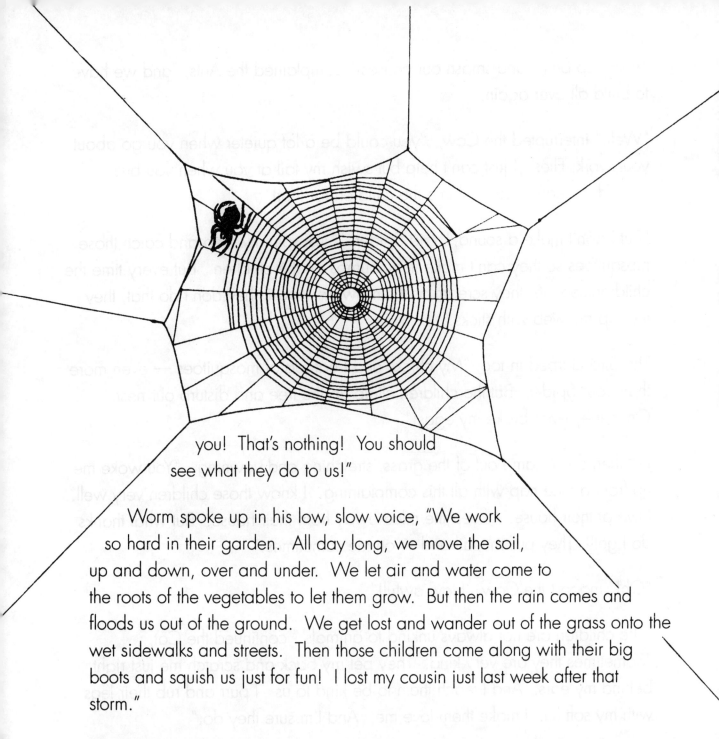

you! That's nothing! You should
see what they do to us!"

Worm spoke up in his low, slow voice, "We work
so hard in their garden. All day long, we move the soil,
up and down, over and under. We let air and water come to
the roots of the vegetables to let them grow. But then the rain comes and
floods us out of the ground. We get lost and wander out of the grass onto the
wet sidewalks and streets. Then those children come along with their big
boots and squish us just for fun! I lost my cousin just last week after that
storm."

The Flies and the Ants joined in, "You'd think we insects are nothing! But it
takes a lot of us to clean up their mess. Every time they let their popsicles drip
on the floor, we come in to eat up that sticky mess," buzzed the Flies.

"And when they eat only half their sandwich. It takes a lot of us to finish off
the rest," called the Ants in a chorus. "It sure would be a messy world without
us," they agreed.

"But all those children can think about is to swat us," buzzed the Flies.

"And step on us and smash our houses!" complained the Ants, "and we have to build all over again!"

"Well," interrupted the Cow, "you could be a lot quieter when you go about your work, Flies. I just can't help but swish my tail at you when you buzz around my ears. I can't blame the children for that!"

"But I don't make a sound," said Spider. "I just spin my web and catch those mosquitoes so they can't make itchy bumps on the children. But every time the children see me, they scream and run away. And if they don't do that, they tear up my web with sticks."

The Bird chirped in too, "My chicks and I eat lots of mosquitoes — even more than you, Spider. But the children climb up the tree and disturb our nest. Once they even broke my eggs!"

Just then a cat came out of the grass, stretching and yawning. "You woke me up from a nice nap with all this complaining. I know those children very well. I live at their house. I keep the mice away from their house. But what thanks do I get? They pull my tail and sit on me sometimes."

"Oh!" mooed the Cow, "How awful!"

"The children are not always unkind to animals," continued the Cat, "Sometimes they are very kind. They pet my back and scratch me just right behind my ears. And I teach them to be kind to us. I purr and rub their legs with my soft fur. I make them love me. And I'm sure they do."

LESSON PLAN 13, STORY A: Kindness to Animals

TOPICS: Science, Animals, Kindness, Obeying, Respect for Elders.

This pair of stories may be most effectively used to accompany a unit on animals. There are many crossover possibilities for science and literature.

LEVEL I (COMPREHENSION)

1. Discuss what the boy was doing that Ibn Umar did not like.

2. Ask what Ibn Umar told the boy's father. Where did Ibn Umar learn not to tie an animal and kill it? Who taught him?

3. What did the Prophet say about animals? Discuss some examples of the behavior the Prophet forbade with this statement. (like putting an animal in a cage and hurting it, or in a trap, or putting insects in a jar and teasing them, or chasing fish in an aquarium.)

LEVEL II (ANALYSIS AND VALUE BUILDING)

1. Ask the children whether animals have feelings or not. If they don't know, draw them into thinking by asking if they see or hear, and what they do when frightened. What do rabbits, squirrels or birds do when we approach them? If they run, it means they are frightened, so they show the feeling of fear, etc.

2. Ask how an animal would feel if we caught it and did something to harm it. Ask how a child would feel if someone held and tried to hurt him or her.

3. Ask the children what we can do to be kind to animals. How can we show them kindness. (putting out food for them, putting up birdhouses, keeping their cages clean if they are pets, stroking their fur or feathers if they let us near, etc.)

4. Discuss how animals become tame or learn to trust us when we are kind to them. Ask the children to tell from their experience how pets or other animals show feelings of trust, anger, affection for the treatment given them. (growling, purring, running away, rubbing legs, staying near, playing with people)

LEVEL III (REINFORCEMENT ACTIVITIES)

It may be best to discuss both stories and combine some of the activities from Stories A and B, with the exception of the worksheet activities. These also combine well with science activities.

1. Put up a birdfeeder near the classroom window, or make feeders for home use, or make hanging seedcakes. (Instructions for both are readily available in the children's section of the library.) The class might go to a pet farm, feed ducks or pigeons at a park, or put out food for squirrels.

2. The class might start an ant farm to observe ant behavior, or hatch baby chicks and care for them, or get a classroom pet to take care of, such as a hamster, turtle or fish.

3. Visit a farm in the spring season and have the guide explain how animals help us in many ways, how their young are cared for, etc.

4. The children might dictate or write about a pet they have at home, and draw a picture of it, telling or illustrating what they do to care for the pet.

LESSON PLAN 13, STORY B: The Animals Complain

TOPICS: Science, Animals, Kindness, Obeying, Respect for Elders, Charity (to animals).

This story has been told successfully using pictures of the animal characters mounted on cardboard with wooden handles. The children make the appropriate animal sounds or motions when the character appears, then stop to hear the dialogue.

LEVEL I (COMPREHENSION)

1. Ask the children to name all the animals in the story. Write their names and post their pictures on the wall or blackboard. [See Worksheet #5, "How do these animals help us?" to identify their contributions.]

2. Ask the children to tell what each animal does for us, as mentioned in the story. Post the picture of this activity beside each picture. An alternate method for #1 and #2 would be to post all the pictures and let the children name and match them.

3. Discuss the animals' complaints. What did the children do to each of the animals in the story? It may be necessary to go back over parts of the story.

4. Talk about which animals in the story are wild, and which live with people. (cow, hens and cat vs. insects, worms, bird)

LEVEL II (ANALYSIS AND VALUE BUILDING)

1. Elicit the children's experience with animals, whether they were frightened of them (dogs, cats, mice, bees, spiders), curious and happy (baby rabbits, fish, hamsters, turtles), disgusted (worms, bugs), or which ones they find cute or ugly.

2. Discuss how animals might see people, and their possible feelings. Portray with some drama how a very small creature might view a very large child looking at it. At this point, the teacher may wish to discuss the reality/unreality aspect of "talking animals" in the story and differentiate between animals' real ability to communicate given them by Allah and the ability to speak given them so often by storytellers.

3. Poll the children on who has ever killed an insect and why, (scared of it, want to get rid of it, just for "fun") Elicit experiences with other animals — did they avoid it, try to approach it, pet it, feed it, ride it, or bother it?

4. Tell the story from the Qur'an about Prophet Sulaiman and the ants, and about the benefits of the bee in Surat al-Nahl, and even about the flies and gnats mentioned in the Qur'an as creatures of Allah whom He cares about and cares for. Explain how everything Allah created has a reason for being alive and a special job to do on the earth.

5. Discuss with the children why it is wrong to kill just for fun, and discuss when it is all right to kill sometimes. (danger from a wild or sick animal or insect; for food after saying "Bismillah" and doing it as kindly as possible)

LEVEL III (REINFORCEMENT ACTIVITIES)

1. Do Worksheet #5, "How do these animals help us?", color. Or collect magazine pictures of the animals mentioned in the story to make a poster showing what they do for us as described. Arrange the pictures in columns and have the children draw lines connecting the animal helper with his job.

2. Use the story to illustrate a science unit on animal homes and animal helpers. Make worksheets for animal homes and animal foods as in #1, as well as other food we get from animals. In particular, bees and honey might be mentioned in connection with Islamic references from Qur'an and Hadith. How do the children react to bees? If they were in the story, would they complain, too?

3. Have the children make masks and insect costumes from paper bags, pipe cleaners, etc., to represent the characters. Let them act out the dialog in the story.

4. Read stories from Love All Creatures(Islamic Foundation) on kindness to animals, as well as other animal stories from the authentic Islamic sources, such as The Whale of Jonah, The Elephant of Abraha, and The Hoopoe of King Soloman (Ahmad Baghat, Shorouk International).

5. Have the children go outside and observe familiar animals and insects. Dig in the ground to find worms, in season, and discuss what they do. [See other activities from Story A.] What may not be observed can be filled in through non-fiction books at the library.

How Do These Animals Help Us?

Draw a line from the animal to how it helps us.

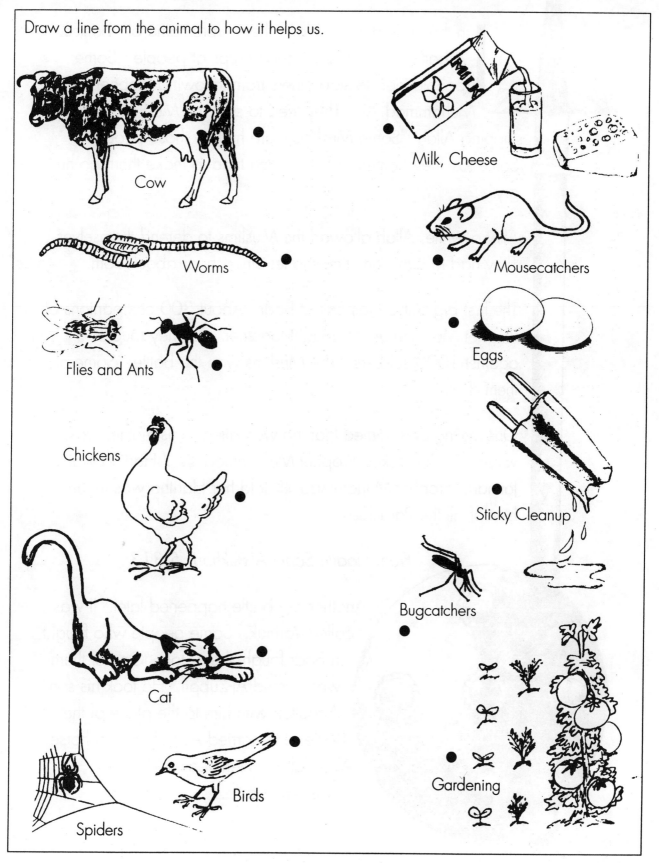

Cow

Worms

Flies and Ants

Chickens

Cat

Spiders

Birds

Milk, Cheese

Mousecatchers

Eggs

Sticky Cleanup

Bugcatchers

Gardening

Defending Islam

In the early days of Islam, there were some big battles. A battle is a fight between groups of people. Some people tried to stop others from following Prophet Muhammad ﷺ. They tried to stop the Muslims from worshipping Allah. Some Muslims were hurt by those people. Some lost their homes. People even tried to make them go hungry.

After a while, Allah allowed the Muslims to defend themselves. They had to fight sometimes to let others hear about Islam.

The first big battle was called Badr. About 300 companions of Prophet Muhammad ﷺ fought together. But they fought against 1000 soldiers. The Muslims won the battle. Some of them died.

One young boy named Haritha was killed. His mother was very sad. She asked Prophet Muhammad ﷺ if Haritha was in Jannah. Prophet Muhammad ﷺ told her Haritha was in the best of all the Paradises.

From Hadith Sahih Al-Bukhari, 5:313

Another big battle happened later. It was called Yarmuk. Some people who fought in Badr fought there, too. One of them was named Al-Zubair. He took his son Abdullah with him to the place of the battle. He carried Abdullah on a horse. Abdullah was ten years old. He watched the battle.

Al-Zubair was hurt at Badr, and then he got better. He had two scars on his shoulder. Another son, named 'Urwa, said he remembered those scars. He used to touch them when he hugged and played with his father.

From Hadith Sahih Al-Bukhari, 5:318; 5:67

Our Uncle From Palestine

We are a Muslim family. We live in the United States. My name is Amina. I go to an Islamic school. I am in kindergarten. My brother Yunus is three years old. We have a baby brother, too.

Our Uncle Amin just came to our house for a visit. He came on an airplane from Palestine. After Papa picked him up from the airport, we had dinner. Uncle Amin talked about our cousins in Palestine. He said that they were having a lot of trouble. He talked about soldiers. I did not understand very much.

When it was time for us to go to bed, I asked our Mama some questions. I asked her about what Uncle Amin said when we were eating dinner. "What is it like in Palestine? Is it far away? Why are they having trouble?"

Mama held the baby and said, "Let me tell you a story about our country,

Palestine."

"Palestine is a land where the holy city of Jerusalem is found. Palestine is a land where many prophets walked. Long ago, Allah brought Prophet Muhammad ﷺ to Jerusalem. He flew him there for a visit in one night. There were no airplanes then, but nothing is difficult for Allah. Later, the Muslims built a masjid on the place where Prophet Muhammad ﷺ stepped."

"Now, some people have come and given the land a new name, Israel. They brought soldiers. They want the Palestinian people to leave the land so they can live there. The soldiers make many problems for the Palestinians. It is very hard for your cousins and their friends. It is hard for their parents."

"What kind of trouble do the soldiers make?" I asked. "Uncle said we should send back some toys and clothes for our cousins. They don't have as much as we do."

"Yes," said Mama, "and Uncle Amin told us bad news. He said that the soldiers came with a bulldozer and smashed the house of your aunt and her family. Now they are living with your uncle. They don't have enough room in the house for everyone. One of your cousins was taken away by the soldiers. They don't know when he will come back."

"Where did they take him?" I asked.

"To a place called a prison. They said he was throwing stones at the soldiers."

"Did he do that?" I asked.

"I don't know, but people are very angry at the soldiers. Sometimes they close the schools and stores where people buy food. Sometimes everyone is told to stay at home for many days."

"Why do the soldiers do those things?" I asked.

"The soldiers want the Palestinian people to leave. Then they want to take all the land and houses for themselves."

"But that is very bad!"

Mama held the baby tight and said, "There are many places in the world where Muslims and other people are in trouble. Some people are not kind to others. They sometimes act selfish and mean."

"What can we do?"

"Muslims must help each other. They must pray for each other to Allah. They must share what they have. They must learn about each other and try to help. And we should thank Allah for what we have. Some people do not have the things we enjoy."

Mama kissed me and said, "Go to sleep, and pray for Muslims everywhere."

Illustration by Palestinian children from Kamal Boullata, Faithful Witnesses: Palestinian Children Recreate Their World (Olive Branch Press, 1990).

LESSON PLAN 14, STORY A Defending Islam

TOPICS: Defending Islam, Family, Parents, Respect for Elders, Belief in Allah, Worshipping Allah, Obeying, Courage and Bravery, History.

This lesson is about the situation of children who lived long ago when Islam first came and the Muslims had to defend their belief. Together with Story B, this lesson is also about Muslims in other parts of the world where life is not as comfortable and easy as many modern children know it. It is also intended to deal with the concept of when it is permissible to fight in defense of something important.

PRE-READING ACTIVITY

1. Introduce the story by reviewing what the children know about the time when Islam first came to Prophet Muhammad. Introduce the idea of resistance to Islam by reminding the students of Lessons 2A and 3A, about people's reaction to Ibrahim's message. Explain how many members of Muhammad's own family, like Ibrahim's own father, did not want to believe in Allah. And, just as the people tried to burn Ibrahim when the idols were broken, many of the first Muslims were punished for believing in Allah and worshipping Him.

2. Explain what a battle is, and why the early Muslims had to fight. (See Level III, Activity #1 below for related stories.)

LEVEL I (COMPREHENSION)

1. Discuss how people have prevented Muslims from worshipping as they wish, first in the time of Prophet Muhammad, then relating these stories briefly to modern incidents in the news at present. [See Level III, Activity #1 below for related stories.]

2. Talk about the role that children might have played in the battle long ago. (Carrying water, flags, beating drums, helping with injured soldiers together with their mothers, taking care of riding and pack animals, carrying father's or brother's shield and armor, etc.)

3. What happened to Haritha in the story? (He was killed.) Where did Prophet Muhammad tell his mother that Haritha went. (He told her that Haritha went to the best of all paradises.)

4. Who was Abdullah's father? (Al-Zubair) Where did Abdullah go with his father? (He rode on the back of his horse to the battle.) Did he fight in the battle? (No, he watched.)

5. What happened to Al-Zubair in the battle of Badr? (He got cut on his shoulder.) What did his other son 'Urwa remember? (He touched the scars when he played with his father.) The teacher may need to clarify what a scar is, and explain that big injuries sometimes leave scars for a long time. They may compare some of their own cuts and scrapes which usually disappear in a few weeks or months. (See Level III, Activity #3 below.)

LEVEL II (ANALYSIS AND VALUE BUILDING)

1. Gather the children's opinions about fighting as a positive or negative activity. Ask them what they think people fight about. What do children fight about sometimes? (toys, space, not taking turns, not sharing, wanting to be first and only, etc.) Explain that Muslims are not allowed to fight over having things in a selfish way.

2. Remind the students of the Ibrahim stories and how some people were angry with Ibrahim because he told them to worship Allah only. They wanted to keep worshipping idols and doing what they were used to. They didn't want Ibrahim to tell others about Allah. Explain that the same thing happened to Prophet Muhammad (S), and people tried to make him stop speaking about Islam. They tried to kill him and people who followed him. Tell the children that Allah allowed the Muslims to fight against these people. But first they had to be patient for a long time.

3. Discuss with the students what happens when people fight, that they often get hurt and even die. The battle is often very frightening, so people need to be very brave, and their families need to be very brave, too. Explain that Muslims are told in the Qur'an that even if they die, Allah will give them Jannah if they fight in a way that He allows.

4. Discuss the feelings of fear and courage, sadness and hope that people have when their families and neighbors are fighting battles. Discuss how Allah helps those people to be strong when they are fighting for what is right and good. Some stories from The Courageous Children (below) will help to illustrate these ideas.

5. Discuss how Al-Zubair showed that he loved his two sons, taking them with him and playing with and hugging them. How did Haritha's mother show her love for her son? (by being very sad and very brave when he died) Explain that Allah is pleased when parents show love to their children, and when children show love to their parents.

LESSON PLAN 14, STORY A Defending Islam

TOPICS: Defending Islam, Family, Parents, Respect for Elders, Belief in Allah, Worshipping Allah, Obeying, Courage and Bravery, History.

LEVEL III (REINFORCEMENT, ENRICHMENT AND EVALUATION ACTIVITIES)

1. Read stories about conduct in battle at the time of Prophet Muhammad and the Sahaba from Stories of Sirah (A. and T. Ghazi, Iqra Foundation), True Stories for Children (M.W. Muhammad, TaHa Publishers), The Courageous Children (A. Scott, Islamic Foundation), Marvellous Stories from the Life of Muhammad (S) (M.A. Tarantino, Islamic Foundation), Love Your God and The Kingdom of Justice (K. Murad, Islamic Foundation), and others.

2. Show the children a globe, telling them where Prophet Muhammad lived and where the Islamic message first came. Then show them the area where the majority of Muslims live, across Africa and Asia. Then explain that Muslims have now come to live in nearly every country in the world, even where most of the people are not Muslims.

3. Show pictures of the kind of equipment used to fight battles in the time of Prophet Muhammad and the Sahaba. Discuss what sort of injuries a fighter would have gotten with these weapons (mostly swords). Ask the children to describe battle equipment now, as they understand it. Compare and contrast, based on the children's knowledge.

4. Make a model of a soldier in the time of Prophet Muhammad for classroom display, including his dress, weapons, and his mount (camel, horse or on foot), using illustrated library books for reference. The teacher will need to do most of the work, but it could be done as a lesson in front of the children, going from planning to the completed model in a series of class periods.

LESSON PLAN 14, STORY B: Our Uncle From Palestine

TOPICS: Family, Community Helpers, Fighting for Islam, Bravery and Courage, Charity, Prayers (for others), Tawhid (unity among Muslims)

PRE-READING ACTIVITY

1. Ask the children in the group whether relatives have come to their homes from other places. Poll the class on the names of places where they have relatives. Elicit their memories of visits to those places.

2. Explain that when relatives come for a visit, they bring news of the family far away. Ask what other ways we get news of faraway families. (telephone and letters)

3. Tell the children that this story is about Muslim families whose lives are different from ours, and who have problems different from ours. It tells about helping other Muslims far away.

LEVEL I (COMPREHENSION)

1. Where does the family live? From what country does their uncle come for a visit?

   How is the children's life described by Uncle Amin different from what the children in the class are used to?

2. How are their lives the same?

3. What difficulties does the story tell about?

4. Who is fighting against the people in the story? What do they want to take away from them?

LEVEL II (ANALYSIS AND VALUE BUILDING)

1. Do the children think that the soldiers frighten the children in Palestine? Compare this with what children in the class are afraid of.

2. What does it mean to be brave? How can we tell if someone has courage? Discuss hypothetical situations of children as described by Mama in the story, relating ideas of fear, bravery and courage.

3. How can we help children in places where fighting is going on? (write letters to help them be brave, ask our families to send food or money, and meet with important people to talk about other ways to help) Suggest to the children that they ask their parents to save some money by not buying a certain toy, or ice cream or similar item and to donate that money. Talk about the idea of not having something you don't really need in order to help someone who doesn't have what they need. Discuss the idea of sacrifice, or giving up something. This could become a broader discussing involving ideas about sacrifice in daily family life.

LEVEL III (REINFORCEMENT, ENRICHMENT AND EVALUATION ACTIVITIES)

1. Using books, magazines and newspapers, show pictures of places in the world where Muslims have a difficult time because of war, hunger, poverty and sickness, but not of the gorey variety which would unduly frighten the children. Use a globe to point out where these Muslims live. You may also show pictures of other children and families who are not Muslim but who suffer from these things. Ask the children to name things that they need, such as food, houses, toys, doctors, etc.

2. Building on Activity #1, above, ask the students to think about some things that they have which are lacking to the children and families pictured. Have them draw pictures of some of these things, then use the pictures to make a group list.

3. Make a bulletin board or posters of some places where Muslims are in need, showing pictures of some things that they need connected by strings to the needy people.

4. Work with the parents to organize a drive to collect food, clothing or money for a particular group.

5. Organize a project with parents, older students or within the class to have the children dictate letters to a government official or other organization about helping Muslims in a troubled area.

A Nice Present

Um Khalid bint Khalid came from a country called Ethiopia. The Prophet sent some of the Muslims there. They were safe from danger there. When they came back, Um Khalid was a little girl who came with them. The Prophet was happy to see them. He was happy to see a little girl like Um Khalid from Ethiopia.

One day the Prophet received a present. He was given some clothes. He liked to share his presents. He looked at one nice dress and asked, "To whom shall we give this to wear?" No one answered, so the Prophet called for little Um Khalid. He told her to wear it. He put his hands on the pretty designs on the dress and said to her "Sanah! Sanah!" He told her it was pretty. He spoke to her in the Ethiopian language.

From Hadith Sahih Al-Bukhari 5:214; 7:713

New Neighbors

Some children are busy playing in front of their house. A girl is watching them from the front porch of her house. She is their new neighbor. They go up to the house and try to talk to her. They ask her to come and play, but she doesn't answer.

Her mother comes to the door. She is wearing a scarf. One of the children says, "She is a Muslima! She wears a scarf like our mom! So he calls to the neighbor, "Salamu 'alaikum!"

She answers, "'Alaikum Salam! My daughter's name is Amina. She speaks Arabic. She doesn't know English yet. Can you help her to learn?"

The children answer, "We know some Arabic. We are learning Arabic at school. We can help her."

Amina's mother spoke to her. She said, The children want you to play, too." Amina goes with them, but she is shy. She doesn't understand what they are saying. The children want her to feel good.

One of the children has an idea. She goes inside and draws a picture for Amina. She comes running out to show her. She points to the picture and says, "Jameela! Jameela!" Amina is very happy with her new Muslim friends.

LESSON PLAN 15, STORY A: A Nice Present

TOPICS: Charity, Gifts and Giving, Guests, History (life long ago), Kindness, Manners, Neighbors, Politeness, Sharing, Serving Others.

LEVEL I (COMPREHENSION)

1. Where did Um Khalid come from? How did she come to the Prophet with the Muslims? As an option, the teacher may discuss how the Muslims went to her country to be safe from danger. It might be useful to recall the Ibrahim story in Lessons #2 and #3 and how his people reacted.

2. What present did Prophet Muhammad (S) receive?

3. Did Prophet Muhammad (S) keep the present for himself?

4. To whom did he want to give the nice dress? (He offered it to anyone, but no one answered. Then he called for Um Khalid.)

5. What did Prophet Muhammad (S) say to Um Khalid? What does it mean in her language?

LEVEL II (ANALYSIS AND VALUE BUILDING)

1. Draw together the conclusions reached from level I discussion and summarize how the little girl was in a strange country with a strange language. Talk about how people feel when they are in a new place and they don't understand. Some of the children may have had such an experience.

2. Ask the children what Prophet Muhammad (S) did to make Um Khalid feel welcome and good. (He gave her a present and he spoke kind words to her in her own language.)

3. Discuss the idea of sharing when we get a present. Ask what we might do if we received a big box of chocolate or cookies.

4. What should we do if we receive a present while other people are with us, but it is not a large amount? (keep it for later, or share even a small amount, or give all it to someone else??) Discuss with various examples of food, toys or clothing.

LEVEL III (REINFORCEMENT ACTIVITIES)

Combine with those for Story B.

1. Read other stories about sharing and neighbors, such as relevant selections from Stories from the Sirah (Iqra Publications) and Love Your Brother, Love Your Neighbor (Islamic Foundation), and expand these ideas.

LESSON PLAN 15, STORY B: New Neighbors

TOPICS: Charity, Gifts and Giving, Guests, History (life long ago), Kindness, Manners, Neighbors, Politeness, Sharing, Serving Others.

LEVEL I (COMPREHENSION)

1. Ask how the children knew that the girl was their new neighbor. What did they do to try to meet her?

2. How did they find out that their new neighbors are Muslims?

3. Why didn't Amina talk to the children? Did the children know how to speak Arabic?

4. How did the children make Amina feel welcome and happy?

LEVEL II (ANALYSIS AND VALUE BUILDING)

1. Talk about being new in a class or a neighborhood, and how someone feels as a stranger. Discuss what we can do to make a new person feel good and comfortable.

2. Ask if the children have ever wanted to play with some other children, but they didn't know them. How did they feel? Did the other children invite them or not? How did they feel in either case?

3. Discuss the feeling of shyness, whether and when it is a good feeling. When does it keep us from doing things we want to do? Does being shy sometimes keep us from doing things we shouldn't do?

4. Identify who neighbors are (people who live near us), and discuss things we should (visiting, helping, being kind and generous to, not disturbing) and should not do (destroying their property, disturbing, ignoring, abusing with speech, etc.) in order to live well together. Ask whether the children's neighbors are Muslim where they live. Explain that we must be good to neighbors no matter who they are. [Discuss the example of the Sunna, especially the story of the neighbor who was unkind to him, throwing garbage on his doorstep; when the man became ill and was unable to throw the garbage, Prophet Muhammad (S) went to his home to ask about him. The man later became a good Muslim.] See reading selections from Story A, III, #1, above.

5. It may be possible to extend the idea of neighbors in the children's awareness to the people of other countries in the world, to the idea that everyone in the world must act as neighbors, and even to the natural environment (animal neighbors).

LEVEL III (REINFORCEMENT ACTIVITIES)

1. Role play a new person coming into the class.

2. Poll the children to know what languages are spoken at their homes. Try to get the children to name simple things in those languages. Speak a foreign language for the children, or bring in a guest speaker to talk about other languages. Gather the children's experiences with English, Arabic and other languages.

3. Listen to songs in other languages, and perhaps learn one, like "Frere Jacque" in French and English, or bring a Spanish speaking child to teach a song to the children. If there is sufficient ethnic variety in the class, Muslim children of Ind Pakistani, African, European and other backgrounds may teach songs from their language, or parents may assist in same.

4. Find out if the children know of someone in the class or the school who just moved into their neighborhood or school community. The class can make up a welcome basket of cookies, paper or real flowers, draw pictures or make welcome cards for the family or families, etc.

5. If level II discussion point #4 has been pursued, the class might use a globe or map of the world's countries to talk about neighboring countries and their peoples, or the idea that the whole world is a neighborhood of countries and peoples. Point out on the globe the countries of origin of children in the class.

NOTES